D1070818

Chemistry

Understanding Substance and Matter

THE STUDY OF SCIENCE

Chemistry

Understanding Substance and Matter

Edited by Russell Kuhtz

Britannica
Educational Publishing

IN ASSOCIATION WITH

ROSEN
EDUCATIONAL SERVICES

Published in 2015 by Britannica Educational Publishing (a trademark of Encyclopædia Britannica, Inc.) in association with The Rosen Publishing Group, Inc.
29 East 21st Street, New York, NY 10010

Distributed exclusively by Rosen Publishing.
To see additional Britannica Educational Publishing titles, go to rosenpublishing.com.

First Edition

Britannica Educational Publishing
J. E. Luebering: Director, Core Reference Group
Anthony L. Green: Editor, Compton's by Britannica

Rosen Publishing
Hope Lourie Killcoyne: Executive Editor
Kathy Campbell: Senior Editor
Nelson Sá: Art Director
Nicole Russo: Designer
Cindy Reiman: Photography Manager
Amy Feinberg: Photo Researcher
Introduction and supplementary material by Kristi Lew

Library of Congress Cataloging-in-Publication Data

Chemistry: understanding substance and matter/edited by Russell Kuhtz.—First edition.
        pages cm.—(The study of science)
Audience: 7-12.
Includes bibliographical references and index.
ISBN 978-1-62275-415-1 (library bound)
1. Chemistry—Juvenile literature. I. Kuhtz, Russell, editor.
QD35.C49 2015
540—dc23

                                                                    2014006448

Manufactured in the United States of America

On the cover: *agsandrew/Shutterstock.com; cover and interior pages borders and backgrounds © iStockphoto.com/ LuMaxArt*

CONTENTS

Students in chemistry class learn that chemistry helps them recognize how the differences in the properties of matter relate to what the matter is composed of. Jon Feingersh/Blend Images/ Getty Images

Why do onions make people cry? What makes fireworks explode? How do rechargeable batteries recharge? All these questions and many more can be answered with one simple word: chemistry. Chemistry plays a very large role in everyday life. Without it, bread would not rise, cleaners would not clean, and life itself would not exist.

Chemistry is the study of matter and the changes that matter undergoes. Anything you can see, touch, smell, or taste is made up of matter. An airplane is matter. An ant is matter. The air that surrounds you is made up of matter, too, although you cannot see it. Matter is anything that has mass and occupies space. Sound and light, though, are not matter. Unlike air, they do not have mass or take up space. A pure substance is matter that has a specific composition and definite properties. Elements and compounds are pure substances, but mixtures, such as apple juice, are not. Apple juice is a mixture of many pure substances, such as water, sugars, and vitamins. The chapters in this book introduce the major concepts of the physical and chemical properties of matter,

including characteristic properties, the use of chemical analysis, and the physical and chemical changes that occur on the molecular level. You will also investigate the classification of matter according to its chemical composition, by element, compound, and mixture.

All matter consists of very small building blocks called atoms. Chemists study how atoms interact with one another. These interactions affect everything—they cause plants to grow, fireflies to glow, and bread dough to rise. They govern how the food you eat is turned into energy, and they are the reason that the leaves on some trees change color in the fall.

Why should you study chemistry? People in many professions, including medicine, environmental science, and marine biology, need a good working knowledge of chemistry. But they are not the only ones. Chemistry is very important in today's society. To be an informed consumer, you need to know what goes into the food you eat, the beverages you drink, and the clothes you wear. Do you know how much fertilizer is needed to make your lawn green and how much is too much? Do you know which household chemicals are safe to combine and which are not? Studying chemistry can help you answer these questions and many others. For this reason, everyone could benefit from knowing a little bit about chemistry and its underlying concepts.

Over time, scientific knowledge builds on itself and the study of chemistry is no exception. The discovery of the atom and the investigation of how atoms interact with one another have changed the world. Chemists today strive to make the world a better place by studying new materials that can make life easier, protect the environment, and provide energy that humans can use.

In this volume, you will be treated to an overview of the history and concepts you may encounter in an introductory chemistry course. People use chemicals every day when they cook, clean, or take medications. Chemical reactions happen all around you as you breathe, eat, or sit to read. As your understanding of chemistry grows, you will see that chemistry helps explain the world you live in, and to varying degrees, we are all chemists.

CHAPTER 1

CHEMISTRY DEFINED

The science of chemistry is the study of matter and the chemical changes that matter undergoes. Research in chemistry not only answers basic questions about nature but also affects people's lives. Chemistry has been used, for example, to make stronger metals, to enrich soil for growing crops, to destroy harmful bacteria, and to measure levels of pollution in the environment. It has also made possible the development of plastics, synthetic fibers, and new medicines.

Products produced by the chemical industry are an ordinary part of our daily lives. The chemical industry converts raw materials, such as water, salt, metals and minerals, petroleum, coal, natural gas, plant cellulose and starch, and atmospheric gases, into other products. Some products require much more processing than others before they are subsequently used by manufacturers and other industries. Manufacturers use chemical products to make metal and

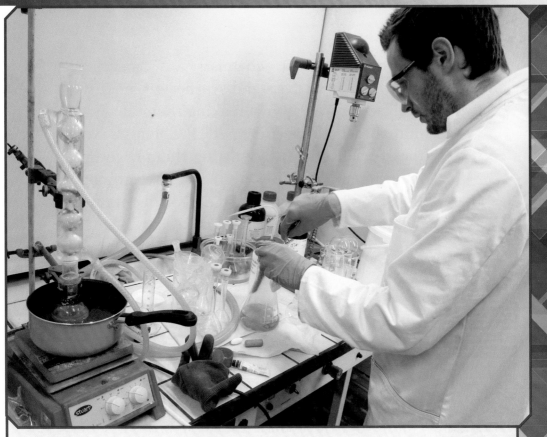

A chemical company's researcher conducts experiments to recover traces of precious metals that are contained in the industrial water that was used during the recycling of electronics. Marc Preel/AFP/Getty Images

paper products; wallboard, pipe, insulation, and other construction materials; polymers for electronic devices, bottles, films, paints, and other items; and fibers for carpets and fabrics. A few examples of other chemical products that are used by consumers include medicines, dyes, paints, fertilizers, shampoos, detergents, waxes, perfumes, cosmetics, and flavorings.

The work of chemistry is generally described as analysis and synthesis. Chemists analyze substances by breaking them down to find out what they are made of. Chemists synthesize substances by putting them together in different, possibly more useful combinations. Assisted by specialized instruments and computers, chemists study materials as small as single atoms and as large and complex as DNA (deoxyribonucleic acid), which contains millions of atoms.

USING CHEMICAL ANALYSIS

Do a criminal suspect's hands show traces of gunpowder? Is the blood sugar level of a person with diabetes under control? Will sulfur and other pollutants be released into the air when a shipment of coal is burned in a power plant? Chemical analysis answers these and many other questions by providing a way to determine the nature of any substance in terms of the elements or compounds that it contains. There are two main approaches to chemical analysis. Qualitative analysis shows which elements or groupings of elements are present in a sample. Quantitative analysis measures how much of each constituent is present. A complete analysis of a substance often requires a combination of these methods.

Scientists first seek to determine whether a sample is organic or inorganic. Organic compounds contain the element carbon, whereas inorganic compounds generally do not contain carbon. One way to distinguish organic and inorganic compounds is by observing the way they behave when they are heated in air. Organic compounds usually melt and then burn with a flame that can be smoky, sometimes leaving a black residue of carbon. Both organic and inorganic compounds are subjected to various tests to determine their makeup.

In the course of the 20th and early 21st centuries, analytical methods evolved considerably. Although traditional methods are still used, most analysis now involves the use of increasingly sophisticated instruments. The older, classical methods rely on chemical reactions to perform an analysis. Newer instrumental methods typically depend on only the measurement of a physical property of a sample, such as a solution's ability to conduct electricity. In some classical methods the results of a chemical reaction need

to be weighed to complete an analysis. This measurement can be made with a balance.

CLASSICAL QUALITATIVE ANALYSIS

The techniques used in qualitative analysis vary depending on the nature of the sample. In some cases it is necessary only to detect the presence of certain elements or groups of elements. In those cases specific tests such as flame tests or spot tests may be applied directly. If, however, all the unknowns in a complex mixture must be identified, a more detailed analysis must be undertaken.

FLAME TESTS

Certain inorganic elements can be identified by the characteristic color that they impart to a flame. To test for this, a portion of the sample is first dissolved in water or acid. A platinum wire is dipped into the solution and then applied to the flame. The resulting color of the flame can indicate the presence of a particular element. A sample of potassium, for example, will produce a violet flame; sodium, bright yellow; calcium, yellow-red; and copper, bright green. When the flame is observed through a device called a spectroscope, which separates a light source into its wavelengths, fine distinctions can be made. The subtle shades that characterize such rare metals as indium, thallium, and cesium were discovered by means of this instrument.

SPOT TESTS

A spot test may be carried out using a glass slide, a porcelain plate, or a piece of laboratory filter paper. A drop or two of a sample in solution is mixed with a chemical preparation, or reagent, that reacts

When a sample of the element strontium (Sr) is subjected to a flame test, the flame burns brilliant red. Charles D Winters/Photo Researchers/Getty Images

in a specific way—typically by changing color or precipitating a solid—if the suspected element is present. Such tests are often used to confirm a suspicion or a tentative result.

WET TESTS

After preliminary tests have been completed on an inorganic compound, a water solution of the sample may be chemically analyzed for the presence of specific ions (charged atoms or groups of atoms). The sample solution is treated with a series of chemicals, each of which separates a certain group of unknown substances from the sample. Each group is then treated with another series of chemicals that divides it into smaller groups or single unknowns. When an unknown has been isolated, it is further tested to confirm its identity. Sometimes a quantitative analysis is also performed to find out how much of the unknown is present. Different series of tests are performed on separate portions of sample solution to detect cations (positively charged ions) and anions (negatively charged ions).

CLASSICAL QUANTITATIVE ANALYSIS

Physical or chemical methods may be used in quantitative chemical analysis. Both approaches employ an analytical balance to weigh samples and precipitates. Balances used in ordinary work can detect differences in mass of 0.1 milligram (0.000004 ounce). For microanalysis of very small samples, balances of much higher sensitivity are available. Physical methods involve the measurement of physical properties such as density (mass per unit volume), refractive index (extent to which the sample solution bends a light beam), or absorption of light. Chemical methods depend on various chemical reactions. The major types of chemical methods are gravimetric and volumetric.

GRAVIMETRIC ANALYSIS

In gravimetric analysis, a chemical reaction separates a selected component from a sample solution. The amount of the component is then calculated from the weight of the separated substance.

Given the task of measuring the quantity of chloride ions (negatively charged chlorine atoms) in a sample solution, for example, a chemist can add a solution of silver nitrate ($AgNO_3$) to the sample. This precipitates the chloride in the form of highly insoluble silver chloride ($AgCl$). The silver nitrate solution is added to the sample solution until no more

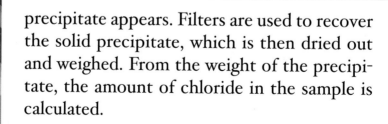

The instrument seen here is an analytical balance, which can be used in gravimetric analysis. It very precisely measures the mass of a precipitate that is at room temperature and even accounts for such factors as dust and airflow. Charles D Winters/Photo Researchers/Getty Images

precipitate appears. Filters are used to recover the solid precipitate, which is then dried out and weighed. From the weight of the precipitate, the amount of chloride in the sample is calculated.

DENSITY

Every substance has its own unique value for density. This physical property is defined as the ratio of mass to volume of a substance. A lead block has more mass than the same volume of aluminum. Thus, the density of lead is greater than that of aluminum. Density also applies to liquids. To have the same mass of water and rubbing alcohol, a greater volume of alcohol is needed because it is less dense than water.

The density of any material can be determined by dividing the mass by the volume. Generally mass is measured in grams (g) and volume in cubic centimeters (cm^3) or milliliters (mL); a cubic centimeter is equal to a milliliter. Density offers a convenient means of obtaining the mass of an object from its volume or vice versa: the mass is equal to the volume multiplied by the density, while the volume is equal to the mass divided by the density. The weight of an object, which is usually of more practical interest than its mass, can be determined by multiplying the mass by the acceleration of gravity.

Density tells much about how particles are arranged in materials. For example, the density of air at sea level is 0.0013 g/cm^3, whereas the density of copper metal is 8.96 g/cm^3. The low density of air and other gases can be explained in terms of the large spaces between their particles. In solids the particles are closely packed, and so the density is higher. The density of solids can vary greatly. For example, the density of gold is 19.3 g/cm^3. Clearly atoms of gold are heavier than atoms of copper. The densest naturally occurring chemical element, osmium (atomic number 76), has a density of 22.6 g/cm^3.

Density explains why some objects float while others sink. Objects that are less dense float in a liquid that is denser.

(continued on the next page)

For example, oil will float on water because its density is less than that of water. A large steel ship also floats on water: Even though steel is denser than water, most of the ship is filled with air, which is less dense than water. Therefore the overall density of the ship is less than that of the water, causing it to float.

VOLUMETRIC ANALYSIS

In volumetric analysis, the volume occupied by the selected component is measured. The volumetric method called titration makes use of a solution of known concentration, called the titrating reagent, that reacts in a certain way with the component under analysis. A graduated vessel called a burette is used to add measured amounts of titrating reagent to a sample until all the component in the sample has reacted with it. A chemical indicator or an electrical test can be used to determine when this point, called the equivalence point, has been reached.

The same kind of chloride sample that was analyzed by a gravimetric method above can also be analyzed by titration. In this method the chemist titrates a sample solution with a silver nitrate solution. The silver ions in the silver nitrate solution combine with the chloride ions in the sample. The sample solution is first treated with an indicator, potassium chromate (K_2CrO_4). This compound will react with silver ions to form a red precipitate of silver chromate (Ag_2CrO_4) when there are no more chloride ions present to remove silver ions from the solution. As the silver nitrate reagent is added to the sample solution by titration, the chemist waits for the first trace of red precipitate to appear. This indicates that the equivalence point has been reached. Having monitored the exact volume of titrating reagent expended up to that point, the chemist is able to calculate the quantity of chloride in the sample.

INSTRUMENTAL ANALYSIS

Instrumental procedures and computerization have greatly increased the efficiency with which chemical analysis can be performed. Instrumental methods can be divided into broad categories—spectral, electric, and separatory—according to the property of the unknown material that is to be measured. Many of the methods can be used for both qualitative and quantitative analysis.

SPECTRAL METHODS

These methods employ some form of electromagnetic radiation—radio waves, infrared radiation, visible light, ultraviolet radiation, or X-rays—that is passed through a sample and then measured. Because the wavelengths at which substances absorb radiation depend on their chemical makeup and because the amount of absorbed radiation increases with the concentration of the substances, the measurements give both qualitative and

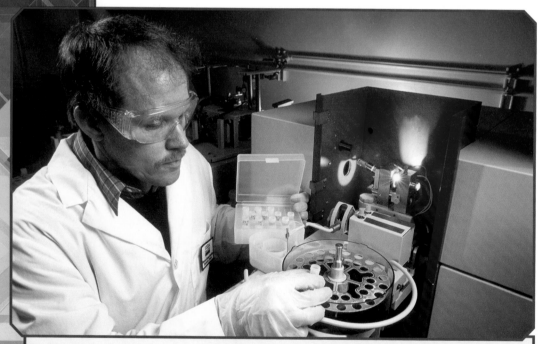

A chemist analyzes a water sample using an atomic absorption spectrophotometer to determine the magnesium content. As the atoms absorb particular wavelengths of light, the spectrophotometer, which measures light intensity, can identify whether certain elements are present. Science Source

quantitative information about the sample. Other spectral methods measure characteristics of radiation reflected (scattered) from the sample or emitted by the sample after it has been excited (put into a higher energy state) by another source of energy, such as electromagnetic rays or particles.

ELECTRICAL METHODS

These methods, also called electroanalysis, make use of electrodes (electrically conductive probes) that are dipped into the sample solution and connected to an instrument that measures some electrical property of the sample—for example, the voltage or current passing through it or its electrical conductivity. The measurements provide qualitative or quantitative information.

SEPARATORY METHODS

Mass spectrometry and chromatography are important separatory methods for chemical analysis. Mass spectrometry directly sorts atoms or molecular fragments into groups. An instrument—either a mass spectrometer or a mass spectrograph—converts the sample into a vapor of ions, accelerates them, and sends

them as a stream through electric or magnetic fields that deflect them along curved paths. The mass and electric charge of each ion determines how much it is deflected. The groups of separated ions are detected electronically or photographically and sometimes collected for further analysis or use. Mass spectrometry is used to analyze inorganic and organic compounds for traces of impurities, to determine the structure of organic compounds, to separate isotopes of elements and measure their relative abundance, and to analyze unknown materials such as meteorites.

Chromatography is an extremely versatile collection of methods for separating chemical substances in a mixture. A chromatographic apparatus has two principal parts, which are in constant contact with each other: a stationary phase of matter and a moving (mobile) phase. The mixture to be separated can be added to the stationary phase or dissolved in the mobile phase. The stationary phase is usually a finely divided solid, a sheet of filter material, or a thin film of a liquid on the surface of a solid. The mobile phase can be a stream of gas or liquid.

Chromatography takes advantage of the fact that each component in a sample mixture has a different relative attraction for the stationary and mobile phases. A component that is more attracted to the mobile phase tends to be moved along with the stream more quickly than one with a greater affinity for the stationary phase. As a result, the individual components are transported farther and farther away from each other as time passes. Often the speed that a component travels gives information about its identity for qualitative analysis.

Very complex mixtures can be separated by chromatography. The method is widely used on chemical compounds of biological origin, such as amino-acid fragments of proteins, complex mixtures of hydrocarbons in petroleum, and volatile mixtures of perfumes and flavors that may contain hundreds of different components.

One of the most common methods is column chromatography. In this method a solution of the sample mixture is poured into the top of a vertical glass column filled with alumina or silica crystals that have been wetted with an inert liquid. As the mixture moves through the column, its various components adhere to the surface of the crystals to a greater or lesser extent, and therefore travel at different rates through the column. Each separated component can then be analyzed qualitatively or quantitatively.

CHAPTER 2

MATTER

An electron, a grain of sand, an elephant, and a giant quasar at the edge of the visible universe all have one thing in common—they are composed of matter. Matter is the material substance that makes up the physical universe. A beam of light, the motion of a falling stone, and the explosion of a stick of dynamite all have one thing in common—they are expressions of energy. Energy and matter together form the basis for all observable phenomena.

Matter itself can be classified according to its physical state: solid, liquid, gas, or plasma. A study of the physical states has led to the conclusion that their characteristics can be explained by assuming that matter consists of particles in motion. This moving-particle theory, called the kinetic-molecular theory of matter, explains many common phenomena, such as the evaporation of liquids and the diffusion of gases. Matter can also be grouped according to the nature of its composition: element, compound, or mixture.

THE STATES OF MATTER

Most of the matter that people ordinarily observe can be classified into one of three states, or phases: solid, liquid, or gas. Solid matter generally possesses and retains a definite size and shape, no matter where it is situated. A pencil, for example, does not change in size or shape if it is moved from a desktop and placed upright in a glass. A liquid, unlike a solid, assumes the shape of its container, even though, like a solid, it has a definite size, or volume. A pint of water changes its shape when it is poured from a glass into a bowl, but

Physical states

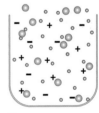

Solid
The molecules that make up a solid are arranged in regular, repeating patterns. They are held firmly in place but can vibrate within a limited area.

Liquid
The molecules that make up a liquid flow easily around one another. They are kept from flying apart by attractive forces between them. Liquids assume the shape of their containers.

Gas
The molecules that make up a gas fly in all directions at great speeds. They are so far apart that the attractive forces between them are insignificant.

Plasma
At the very high temperatures of stars, atoms lose their electrons. The mixture of electrons and nuclei that results is the plasma state of matter.

Four states of matter are pictured here: solid, liquid, gas, and plasma. A fifth state, called Bose-Einstein condensate, was isolated in a laboratory in 1995 and occurs at such an extremely low temperature that atoms do not move at all. Each state is known as a phase. Encyclopædia Britannica, Inc.

its volume remains the same. A gas expands to fill the complete volume of its container.

At a given temperature and pressure, a substance will be in the solid, liquid, or gaseous state. But if the temperature or the pressure changes, its state may also change. At constant atmospheric pressure the state of water, for example, changes with changes in temperature. Ice is water in the solid state. If it is removed from a freezer and placed in a warm pan, the ice warms up and changes to the liquid—water. If the pan is then placed over a hot fire, the water heats up and changes to the gaseous state of water—steam.

Most substances can exist in any of the three states (provided that they do not decompose chemically, as sugar, for example, often does when it is heated in air). Oxygen must be cooled to very low temperatures before it becomes a liquid or a solid. Quartz must be heated to very high temperatures before it becomes a liquid or a gas.

In most people's experience, wide changes in pressure are not as common as drastic changes in temperature. For this reason, examples of the effects of pressure on the states of matter are not common. Often, high-pressure machines and vacuum (low-pressure) machines must be used to study the effects of pressure changes on matter. Under very low pressures, matter generally tends to enter the gaseous phase. At very high pressures, gases tend to liquefy and liquids tend to solidify. In fact, at the very lowest temperatures that can be reached, helium will not solidify unless a pressure of some 25 times normal atmospheric pressure is applied.

The relation between pressure and temperature in changes of state is familiar to people who live at high altitudes. There the pressure is lower than at sea level, so water boils at a lower temperature. Cooking anything in water takes longer on a mountaintop than at sea level.

These properties of the three states of matter are easily observed. They are explained, however, by a theory that describes the behavior of particles far too small to be seen.

ATOMIC THEORY OF MATTER

All substances are made up of tiny units called atoms. Each atom consists of a massive, positively charged center called the nucleus, around which fly one or more negatively charged electrons.

The nucleus itself contains at least one proton, a positively charged particle. In all

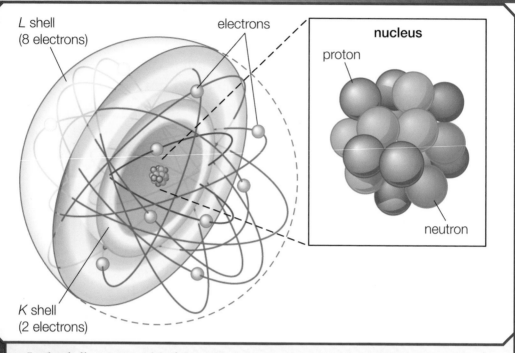

L shell
(8 electrons)

electrons

nucleus

proton

neutron

K shell
(2 electrons)

In the shell atomic model of the noble gas neon, electrons occupy different energy levels, or shells. Its nucleus has 10 protons and 10 neutrons. Chemical properties are explained in terms of how the shells are occupied with electrons. Neon's atomic number is 10, which means that there are 10 electrons in its atom. Two electrons are in the first shell and eight electrons occupy its second, outermost shell, which makes it full. Encyclopædia Britannica, Inc.

atoms except those of ordinary hydrogen, the nucleus also contains at least one neutron, a particle that has no electrical charge. A neutral atom has the same number of electrons as protons, so the electrical charges cancel.

The identity of an atom and its atomic number is determined by the number of protons in its nucleus. For example, there is one proton in the nucleus of a hydrogen atom, so hydrogen has atomic number 1. Oxygen, with eight protons, has atomic number 8; iron has the atomic number 26; and mercury has the atomic number 80.

Substances that are composed of only one kind of atom are called elements. Only 90 elements occur naturally on Earth in significant amounts. The lightest is hydrogen; the heaviest is uranium.

The nuclei of a given element all have the same number of protons but may have a differing number of neutrons. For example, about 99.8 percent of the oxygen nuclei in nature contain eight neutrons as well as eight protons. But a very few oxygen nuclei contain nine neutrons, and some even contain 10 neutrons. Each kind of nucleus is a different isotope of oxygen. Each isotope has a different number of neutrons.

Most hydrogen atoms are made up of a single proton with an electron circling it. However, one isotope of hydrogen contains a neutron as well. This isotope is called deuterium. Because neutrons have approximately the same mass as protons, deuterium atoms have about twice as much mass as those of the ordinary isotope of hydrogen. An extremely rare form of hydrogen, called tritium, has one proton and two neutrons in its nucleus. This is an unstable arrangement, so the tritium nucleus is radioactive. Over time it gives off

a negatively charged particle and changes to a stable helium nucleus with two protons and one neutron.

Many other isotopes of the various elements are radioactive. They can give off radiation of different kinds, changing to other elements or to different isotopes of the same element. Many radioactive isotopes are human-made, produced in nuclear reactors and particle accelerators.

The heaviest element that occurs in significant amounts in nature, uranium, has 92 protons, and its most common isotope has 146 neutrons. Transuranium elements—elements with more protons than uranium—are relatively unstable. Some exist for only a fraction of a second before they decay into other elements. Scientists have synthesized about two dozen of these transuranium elements, a number of which were later found to occur naturally in trace amounts in uranium ores.

Substances that are composed of more than one kind of atom are either compounds or mixtures. The atoms in compounds are joined together chemically. In one type of compound, ions (electrically charged atoms or groups of atoms) are held together; in another type of compound, atoms are joined together to form molecules. This chemical bonding is the result of the electrical forces between the ions or the force of attraction of the electrons of one atom for the nucleus of another atom. For example, in one type of bonding two atoms of hydrogen and one atom of oxygen share electrons and form a water molecule. The chemical symbol for water, H_2O denotes this combination.

The atoms, ions, or molecules in a mixture intermingle with one another but are not joined chemically. Salt water is a kind of mixture called a solution. Salt is composed of ions, and they spread throughout the water when the salt dissolves.

Regardless of whether water is in the solid, liquid, or gaseous state, its molecules always consist of one atom of oxygen and two atoms of hydrogen. Solid water, liquid water, and gaseous water all have the same chemical composition. Instead, the difference between these physical states depends on which energy is larger: the energy associated with the attraction between molecules or the heat energy.

ATOMIC THEORY AND THE STATES OF MATTER

A certain amount of attraction exists between all molecules. If repulsive forces are weaker than these intermolecular attractive forces, the molecules stick together. However, molecules are in constant random motion because of their thermal, or heat, energy. As the temperature of a substance increases, this molecular motion becomes greater. The molecules spread out and are less likely to unite. As the temperature decreases, the motion becomes smaller. The molecules are thus more likely to linger in each other's vicinity and bind together.

In a solid, the intermolecular attractive forces overcome the disruptive thermal energies of the molecules. In most solids the molecules are bound together in a rigid, orderly arrangement called a crystal. These types of solids are called crystalline solids. (In some other solids, such as glasses, gels, and many plastics, the molecules are not arranged in crystals.) Although the molecules in a crystal are held rigidly in place, they still vibrate because of their thermal energy. It may be difficult to think of ice as having heat energy. But even in ice each water molecule, though held firmly in the crystal pattern, vibrates around a fixed position. This vibrational motion is an expression of the thermal energy of ice.

As the temperature of the solid is increased, its molecules vibrate with greater and greater energies until they gain enough vibrational energy to overcome the intermolecular attractive forces. They then break loose from their fixed positions in the crystal arrangement and move about more or less freely. The substance now assumes the shape of its container but maintains a constant volume. In other words, the substance has melted and is now a liquid.

Melting is a change of state, or a phase change. The temperature at which melting takes place varies from substance to substance. Water and iron, for example, melt at different temperatures. The melting temperature remains the same, however, for a given material at a given pressure. At atmospheric pressure water always melts at 32°F (0°C).

Phase changes can work in reverse. If the temperature of a liquid is gradually decreased, a point is eventually reached at which the intermolecular forces are strong enough to bind the molecules despite the disruptive thermal motions. Then a crystal forms: the substance has frozen. The temperature at which this liquid-to-solid phase change takes place is the freezing point. The freezing point of a substance occurs at the same temperature as its melting point.

This theory of matter can also explain the liquid-to-gas change of state, a process called vaporization or evaporation. As heat is applied to a liquid, some molecules gain sufficient thermal energy to overcome the intermolecular

THE FOURTH STATE OF MATTER

At extremely high temperatures atoms may collide with such force that electrons are knocked free from the nuclei. The resulting mixture of free negative and positive particles is not a gas according to the usual definition. Such material is called a plasma. Some scientists consider the plasma state to be a fourth state of matter. Actually, about 99 percent of the known matter in the universe is in the plasma state. In stars matter is hot enough, and in interstellar space it is diffuse enough, for the electrons to be completely separated from the nuclei. From an astronomical standpoint, somewhat unusual conditions exist on Earth, where plasmas are difficult to produce.

attraction—surface tension—exerted by molecules at the surface of the liquid. These high-energy molecules break free from the liquid and move away. Such molecules are now in the gaseous state. As more heat is applied, more molecules gain enough energy to move away until—at a temperature called the boiling point of the liquid—all the molecules can gain enough energy to escape from the liquid state.

The average distance between molecules in the gaseous state is extremely large compared to the size of the molecules, so the intermolecular forces in a gas are quite weak. This

When dry ice, which is solid carbon dioxide (CO_2), sublimes, it changes state to form gaseous carbon dioxide. When a gas changes directly to a solid without going through a liquid phase, it is called deposition. WhiteTag/Shutterstock.com

explains why a gas fills the entire volume of its container. Since intermolecular forces are so small, a gas molecule moves until it strikes either another gas molecule or the container wall. The net effect of the many molecules striking the container walls is observed as pressure.

Sometimes a substance will pass directly from the solid state to the gaseous state without passing through the liquid state. This process is called sublimation. Dry ice (solid carbon dioxide) sublimates at atmospheric pressure. Liquid carbon dioxide can form if

the gas is subjected to over five times atmospheric pressure.

MASS AND WEIGHT

All matter exerts a gravitational attractive force on other matter. The weight of a body is determined by the gravitational forces exerted upon it. A body at Earth's surface experiences a gravitational pull toward the center of the planet. If the body moves farther from Earth's center (to the top of a high mountain, for example), the gravitational force on it decreases, so its weight decreases. If the body moves to a lower point on Earth's surface (into a deep valley, for example), the gravitational force on it increases, so its weight increases. The increase is far greater if the body then moves to the gravitational field of a giant planet, say, Jupiter. A body's weight can change; it varies with the strength of the gravitational field in which the body is placed.

It is important to understand the difference between mass and weight. Although the mass of a body is the same everywhere (it is the measure of the amount of matter in an object), the weight of a body depends upon the strength of the local gravitational field (it is the gravitational force an object experiences because of its mass). An astronaut standing on the surface of the moon weighs less than when standing on Earth, but the astronaut's mass is the same in both places.

Nevertheless, there is a relationship between mass and weight. Mass and weight are proportional to each other. The more mass a body has, the more it will weigh at any given point in space.

ATOMS AND THE ELEMENTS

The tiny units of matter known as atoms are the basic building blocks of chemistry. An atom is the smallest piece of matter that has the characteristic properties of a chemical element, such as hydrogen, oxygen, calcium, iron, gold, and neon. Ninety-eight types of atom exist in nature in at least trace amounts, and each one forms a different element. Elements are made up of only one type of atom—gold contains only gold atoms, and neon contains only neon atoms—but other substances are mixtures of different kinds of atoms. Atoms also join together chemically to form molecules. Matter is made

up of molecules, atoms, and ions (electrically charged atoms or groups of atoms), so atoms are basic components of matter. Since atoms, ions, and molecules are very small, the bulk matter of everyday life consists of large amounts of these components.

The study of matter has helped chemists discover that the whole universe is made up of chemical building blocks called elements. The science of chemistry involves a study of these elements and of the compounds that are formed when different elements combine.

CHAPTER 3

ELEMENTS AND THE PERIODIC TABLE

ny substance that cannot be decomposed into simpler substances by ordinary chemical processes is defined as a chemical element. Ninety elements are found in nature in significant amounts. They are found either chemically free, such as the oxygen in air, or combined with other elements, such as the hydrogen and oxygen in water. Eight more elements exist in nature but only in trace amounts (they are radioactively unstable). Nuclear physics experiments have yielded about 18 heavier elements, also radioactively unstable, that do not exist in nature.

Some substances now recognized as elements—copper, iron, silver, tin, gold, mercury, and lead—were known in ancient times because they are present on Earth in relatively pure form. But they were not then recognized as elements. Early Greek philosophers did believe that there are fundamental substances from which all matter is made, but their understanding

In this 19th-century engraving, Antoine-Laurent Lavoisier is shown during his experiment to determine water's composition by igniting the mixture with an electric spark. In 1783, he reacted oxygen with "inflammable air" (now known as hydrogen), which resulted in water, and he found that water was not an element but a compound of oxygen and inflammable air. Science Source/Photo Researchers/ Getty Images

of those substances varied from the modern definition of an element. The philosopher Thales believed that the essential substance was water, while Heraclitus thought that it was fire. Later Greek thinkers, including Empedocles and Aristotle, believed that there were four elements: earth, air, fire, and water.

One of the first people to define elements in the modern sense was the British chemist Robert Boyle, in 1661. He said that matter was made up of minute corpuscles, or bodies, that differed in their shape and motion. In 1789 the French chemist Antoine-Laurent Lavoisier made the first attempt to list elements based on the modern definition.

NAMING ELEMENTS

Each element has a symbol that is used by chemists around the world as a kind of short-hand. Symbols for elements may have one letter or two. Wherever possible, the symbol is the first letter of the common name or the Latin name of the element. For example, the symbol for hydrogen is H; for carbon, C; for uranium, U. The symbol for potassium is K, after *kalium*, the Latin name for that element.

Since there are not enough single letters to go around and several elements may start with

At left is a sample of the soft, shiny alkali metal potassium. Below, potassium's square from the periodic table of the elements shows its symbol K, atomic number 19, atomic weight 39.0983, and its electron shells (2, 8, 8, 1). Andrew Lambert Photography/ Science Source

the same letter, other letters must sometimes be added. In such cases the symbol is the first letter of the element's name followed by one other letter in the name. For example, helium is He and chlorine is Cl. The Latin name for lead is *plumbum*, and its symbol is Pb. Only the first letter is capitalized in the symbol for an element. Co, which is the symbol for cobalt, is different from CO, which is the chemical formula for carbon monoxide, a compound formed from carbon and oxygen.

ATOMIC PROPERTIES

Chemists also now know that elements are made of atoms. Although the idea that matter was made of atoms had previously existed, it was not until the beginning of the 19th century that physicists and chemists begin to collect the evidence needed to prove the theory and to understand the nature of atoms.

The atomic theory can be summarized as follows: (1) Ordinary matter is made of small particles called atoms. (2) Atoms of the same elements have the same average masses, and atoms of different elements have different average masses. (3) Chemical reactions take place between atoms or groups of atoms.

Chemical elements are classified or identified according to properties of their atoms. Each element has its own type of atoms—hydrogen consists of only hydrogen atoms, and helium consists of only helium atoms. All atoms are composed of three smaller particles: the proton, the neutron, and the electron. Each of these plays a role in defining the element.

ATOMIC NUMBER

The heart of each atom, its nucleus, contains one or more protons, each having a positive

electric charge. The number of protons and thus the number of positive charges varies from one in hydrogen, the lightest element, to more than 100 for the heaviest known elements. This number is known as the atomic number. The atomic number was devised by the English scientist Henry Moseley in 1913. He arranged the elements according to the patterns they produced when struck by X-rays. Later on, his arrangement was shown to coincide with the number of positive charges—protons—in the nucleus.

ISOTOPES

All nuclei except those of ordinary hydrogen contain not only positively charged protons but also neutrons, which are electrically neutral. The number of neutrons can vary in atoms of the same element, but such variations do not affect the number of electrons, the atomic number, or the overall charge on the atom. They affect the chemical properties slightly and also affect the mass of the nucleus and therefore of the atom. Atoms of the same element that vary in mass because of differing numbers of neutrons are called isotopes. The total number of protons plus neutrons is called the mass number of the atom or isotope. This whole number is very close to the atomic mass.

ATOMIC MASS (OR ATOMIC WEIGHT)

An atom has very little mass. One oxygen atom has a mass of only 0.000000000000000000000027 gram. (One gram is equal to 0.035 ounces.) Because such a number is awkward to use, chemists instead use a unit based on an atomic standard of reference, the carbon isotope of mass 12, which is written carbon-12. This is the isotope of carbon that has in its nucleus 6 neutrons in addition to the 6 protons that all carbon atoms possess. One-twelfth of the mass of carbon-12 is defined as the atomic mass unit (amu). In whole numbers, the atomic mass of an atom of hydrogen is 1; of carbon, 12; and of oxygen, 16. Precise atomic masses of elements as found in nature, which are usually referred to as atomic weight, are fractional numbers. Carbon's atomic weight, for example, is 12.011. It takes into account small amounts of carbon-13 and carbon-14 (carbon isotopes with additional neutrons) that are naturally present in addition to carbon-12.

Atomic masses can also be expressed in grams. The resulting number is known as the gram-atomic mass (or gram-atomic weight). It represents the mass in grams of 6.02×10^{23} atoms of the element. For example, 1 gram of hydrogen contains 6.02×10^{23} hydrogen atoms and 12 grams of carbon contains 6.02×10^{23} carbon atoms. The number 6.02×10^{23} is known as Avogadro's number.

ELECTRON SHELLS AND CHEMICAL ACTIVITY

The nucleus of an atom is surrounded by negatively charged electrons. The electrons are arranged in layers called shells. An atom can have as many as seven shells, each of which holds only a certain number of electrons. The shells, in sequence from the closest to the farthest from the nucleus, hold a maximum of 2, 8, 18, 32, 50, 72, and 98 electrons each. The lightest element, hydrogen, has one electron in the first shell. The heaviest elements in their normal states have only the first four shells fully occupied with electrons and the next three shells partially occupied.

If it is an electrically neutral atom, the electrons are equal in number to the protons. Often, however, an atom has either more electrons or fewer electrons than protons and is thus either negatively or positively charged, respectively.

Electrons can be shown by means of dots placed around the chemical symbol for an element. For example:

Li·   ·Be·   ·Ḃ·   ·Ċ·   ·Ṅ·   ·Ö·   ·F̈:   :N̈e:

Usually only the outermost shell is shown, since this is the shell that is involved in chemical activity. If the outermost shell is complete, or filled with the maximum number of electrons for that shell, the atom is electrically stable and inert, with little or no tendency to interact with other atoms. Helium, with two electrons filling its single shell, and neon, with two electrons in its first shell and eight in its second, are both inert.

Atoms with incomplete outer shells seek to fill or to empty such shells by gaining or losing electrons or by sharing electrons with other atoms. This is the basis of an atom's chemical activity. Atoms that have the same number of electrons in the outer shell have similar chemical properties, since their methods of attaining complete outer shells or eliminating incomplete ones are similar.

ELEMENTS FORM GROUPS AND PERIODS

By looking at the atomic masses (atomic weights) of the elements and their chemical properties, chemists discovered that the elements follow a pattern that lets them be organized in a very useful way. The first person to describe this pattern successfully was the Russian chemist Dmitry Mendeleyev (also spelled Dmitri Mendeleev), in 1869.

Mendeleyev noticed that the elements do not change properties gradually, in keeping with gradual increase in atomic weights. Rather, the properties change gradually through a certain number of elements, called a "period." The properties and their pattern of changes recur, or repeat, through the next period. To express this recurrence, Mendeleyev stated the periodic law: the properties of the elements are periodic functions of the atomic weights. The German chemist Julius Lothar Meyer independently reached a similar conclusion.

When the elements are arranged according to the law, the result is the periodic table of the elements. Chemists now know that the periodic law is better expressed in terms of atomic number than in terms of atomic weight, and Mendeleyev's original table has

но въ ней, мнѣ кажется, уже ясно выражается примѣнимость выставляемаго мною начала ко всей совокупности элементовъ, пай которыхъ извѣстенъ съ достовѣрностью. На этотъ разъ я и желалъ преимущественно найдти общую систему элементовъ. Вотъ этотъ опытъ:

		Ti=50	Zr=90	?=180
		V=51	Nb=94	Ta=182
		Cr=52	Mo=96	W=186
		Mn=55	Rh=104,4	Pt=197,4
		Fe=56	Ru=104,4	Ir=198
	Ni=Co=59		Pl=106,6	Os=199
H=1		Cu=63,4	Ag=108	Hg=200
	Be=9,4	Mg=24	Zn=65,2	Cd=112
	B=11	Al=27,4	?=68	Ur=116	Au=197?
	C=12	Si=28	?=70	Sn=118
	N=14	P=31	As=75	Sb=122	Bi=210
	O=16	S=32	Se=79,4	Te=128?
	F=19	Cl=35,5	Br=80	I=127
Li=7	Na=23	K=39	Rb=85,4	Cs=133	Tl=204
		Ca=40	Sr=87,6	Ba=137	Pb=207
		?=45	Ce=92
		?Er=56	La=94
		?Yt=60	Di=95
		?In=75,6	Th=118?

а потому приходится въ разныхъ рядахъ имѣть различное измѣненіе разностей, чего нѣтъ въ главныхъ числахъ предлагаемой таблицы. Или же придется предполагать при составленіи системы очень много недостающихъ членовъ. То и другое мало выгодно. Мнѣ кажется притомъ, наиболѣе естественнымъ составить кубическую систему (предлагаемая есть плоскостная), но и попытки для ея образованія не повели къ надлежащимъ результатамъ. Слѣдующія двѣ попытки могутъ показать то разнообразіе сопоставленій, какое возможно при допущеніи основнаго начала, высказаннаго въ этой статьѣ.

Li	Na	K	Cu	Rb	Ag	Cs	—	Tl
7	23	39	63,4	85,4	108	133		204
Be	Mg	Ca	Zn	Sr	Cd	Ba	—	Pb
B	Al	—	—	—	Ur	—	—	Bi?
C	Si	Ti	—	Zr	Sn	—	—	—
N	P	V	As	Nb	Sb	—	Ta	—
O	S	—	Se	—	Te	—	W	—
F	Cl	—	Br	—	J	—	—	—
19	35,5	58	80	190	127	160	190	220

been rearranged to reflect that idea. Each horizontal row forms a period of elements. Today the lighter elements (with atomic numbers 1 through 20) can be arranged in a table according to their properties as follows:

An early version of Russian chemist Dmitry Mendeleyev's periodic table of the elements. Sovfoto/Universal Images Group/Getty Images

	IA	IIA	IIIA	IVA	VA	VIA	VIIA	0
Period	$_1$H							$_2$He
Period	$_3$Li	$_4$Be	$_5$B	$_6$C	$_7$N	$_8$O	$_9$F	$_{10}$Ne
Period	$_{11}$Na	$_{12}$Mg	$_{13}$Al	$_{14}$Si	$_{15}$P	$_{16}$S	$_{17}$Cl	$_{18}$Ar
Period	$_{19}$K	$_{20}$Ca						

All the elements in each vertical column of the table have similar chemical properties. A column of these related elements forms a group (for example, group 2 [IIA]). The chemical properties depend on the valence electrons in the outermost energy level of an atom. Valence electrons can be lost, gained, or shared, depending on the nature of the element. The alkaline earth metals, for example, have two electrons in their outermost shell, and are labeled with Roman numerals II and an "A," called main group elements. The International Union of Pure and Applied Chemistry, which sets standards for the naming of elements and the periodic table, decided to label the columns to bring the periodic table into accord with the modern understanding of electron structure in atoms. Rather than using Roman numerals with "A" columns and "B" columns (for groups that were not main group elements) and using the Arabic numeral "0," the replacement system simply uses the Arabic numerals 1 through 18.

Not only does this system align more fully with the current understanding of electron arrangement, but it also helped standardize group nomenclature and reduce the confusion caused by scientists using different numbering systems.

THE NOBLE GASES

Six elemental gases are composed of such exceptionally stable atoms that they almost never react with other elements. They are the gases that make up group 18 (0) (the rightmost column) of the periodic table: helium (He), neon (Ne), argon (Ar), krypton (Kr), xenon (Xe), and radon (Rn). When they were first discovered, these gases were thought to be exceedingly rare and completely inactive; thus they were named the rare gases, inert gases, or noble gases (the term "noble," in chemistry and alchemy, had long signified a lack of chemical reactivity).

In 1962, however, Neil Bartlett of the University of British Columbia succeeded in producing a chemical reaction involving a noble gas—a reaction between xenon and fluorine (an extremely reactive gas) that formed the first xenon compound. Since that time, scientists have found that under the proper conditions the other heavy noble gases, radon and krypton, will combine with fluorine as well.

Ordinarily, the noble gases are colorless, odorless, and nonflammable. They are not as rare as originally thought; all occur as minor constituents of the atmosphere, and helium is a component of some natural gases. In fact, with the exception of hydrogen, helium is the most plentiful element in the universe, making up almost 25 percent of its total mass.

The gases' lack of chemical activity has been exploited in a number of commercial uses. In general, they are extracted from the air in a process known as fractional distillation and used to provide an inert, nonflammable atmosphere for such applications as filling lighter-than-air craft; cutting, welding, and refining metals; and growing the pure silicon crystals used in transistors. Some of the gases are used in display, or neon, lighting, fluorescent lighting, and discharge lamps. The helium and argon formed in minerals by radioactive decay can be used to determine the age of certain specimens.

CLASSIFICATION OF ELEMENTS IN THE PERIODIC TABLE

The periodic table provides an easy way to identify related groups of elements. Those elements on the left of the periodic table are base-forming, while those on the right are

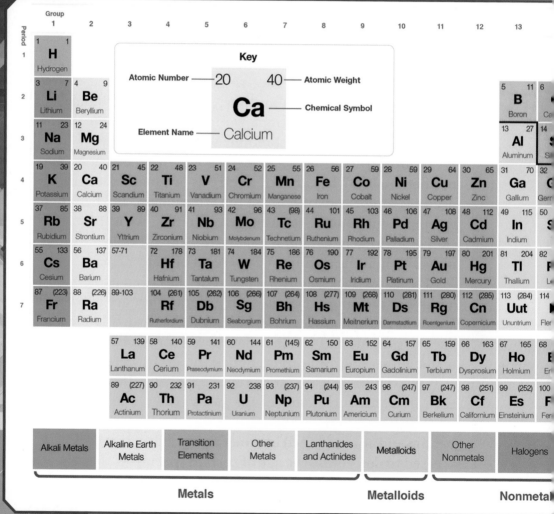

acid-forming. Those in between can be either. The periodic arrangement also divides the elements into metallic and nonmetallic kinds. A distinction is usually made between pure metals and nonmetals according to physical and chemical properties. Of the elements shown in the table at the bottom of page 53, lithium (Li), beryllium (Be), sodium (Na), magnesium (Mg), aluminum (Al), potassium (K), and calcium (Ca) are metallic. The others are nonmetallic.

The periodic table groups elements into chemical families. In the table to the left, for example, the group in the far-right column contains helium (He), neon (Ne), and argon (Ar). These are included in the family of elements called the noble gases. (In some tables this group is labeled "0"; in others, "18" or "VIII.") In group 1 (IA) are hydrogen (H), lithium, sodium, and potassium. Except for hydrogen, these are soft, active substances that act chemically like

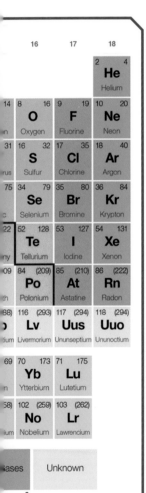

A modern periodic table of the elements displays all the missing gaps from Mendeleyev's era filled in, including the noble gases (group 18) and the artificially created elements such as fermium (Fm), an actinide. Kris Everson

metals in many ways. They react with water to form basic, or alkaline, solutions. Because of these properties they are known as alkali metals. In group 2 (IIA) is the family of elements known as the alkaline earth metals. In group 17 (VIIA) are the halogens. Their compounds with hydrogen, for example hydrogen fluoride (HF) and hydrogen chloride (HCl), dissolve in water to form acids. Hydrogen is sometimes included with the halogens because of certain characteristics it shares with them.

Properties of Metals and Nonmetals

METALS	NONMETALS
Physical Properties	
metallic luster	various appearances
high conductivity for heat and electricity	low conductivity for heat and electricity
ductile	nonductile
Chemical Properties	
form basic solutions	form acidic solutions
form positive ions in solutions	form negative ions in solutions

Many elements with atomic numbers greater than 20 show complicated structures, because they have inner shells of electrons that accept as many as 18 or 32 electrons. Elements having atoms of this type appear in the periodic table as a transition, or inserted, group between groups 2 (IIA) and 3 (IIIA). The electron structures of some of these elements, such as chromium, iron, and nickel, endow their compounds with bright colors. The transition elements include the rare-earth elements and the actinide series.

CHAPTER 4

CHEMICAL REACTIONS

When gasoline is burned, bread is eaten, or plastics are produced from petroleum, chemical changes occur. When a substance undergoes a chemical change, mass is conserved—that is, the amount of mass in the substance is the same before and after the chemical change takes place. The atoms keep their original identity and their number stays the same, but they are rearranged into new combinations. However, the chemical properties of the starting materials vanish, and the properties of the new materials appear. The process by which a substance is changed into another substance is called a chemical reaction.

In addition to chemical change, matter can also undergo two other kinds of

Cheesemakers process a large copper vat of cheese in Beaufort, France. Chemical reactions occur in cheesemaking, when an acid, such as vinegar, or an enzyme, such as calves' rennet, is mixed with cow's milk protein and separates the milk into curds and whey. Jean-Pierre Clatot/AFP/Getty Images

changes—physical and nuclear. The boiling of water, the melting of ice, and the dissolving of table sugar in tea are all examples of physical changes. In all these reactions, the chemical composition of the substances involved remains the same. As with chemical changes, mass is conserved when matter undergoes a physical change. The only change is in physical form.

The phenomenon of radioactivity, the fission of uranium-235, and the fusion of hydrogen atoms (to form helium atoms), with the

Nuclear Fission

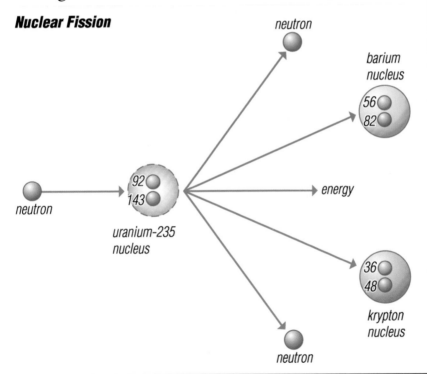

In this picture of nuclear fission, the impact of a low-energy neutron splits the nucleus of the uranium isotope U-235 into two new nuclei. These can be nuclei of any of 30 or more elements ranging in atomic number from 30 to 64. Krypton and barium are the examples shown here. Energy and neutrons are also produced. Encyclopædia Britannica, Inc.

resultant release of nuclear energy, are examples of nuclear changes. In each case the atomic nucleus changes and one kind of atom is transformed into another. The release of nuclear energy in these reactions is associated with the loss of a small amount of nuclear mass.

ELEMENTS, COMPOUNDS, AND MIXTURES

A sample of a pure element contains atoms that are chemically the same but different from those of all other elements. Pure copper contains only copper atoms, pure oxygen only oxygen atoms. The tendency of atoms of different elements to combine makes possible a great variety and number of compounds. A compound is made up of two or more elements that have undergone a chemical change. Hence compounds are composed of two or more kinds of atoms. Such substances as water, sugar, and salt are compounds.

Elements combine, or react, to form compounds that have physical and chemical properties different from those of the original elements. Thus atoms of hydrogen and oxygen, two gases that liquefy only at very low temperatures, unite to form water, a compound that is liquid at room temperature and is unlike either hydrogen or oxygen. Methane gas, made from carbon and hydrogen, and table sugar, made from carbon, hydrogen, and oxygen, are other examples of compounds formed from reactions.

A compound has a definite composition—its constituent elements always occur in the same proportion, or formula. Water, for example, always contains two hydrogen atoms for every oxygen atom. The number of known compounds, both natural and artificial, is in the millions. Countless others remain to be discovered or synthesized in the laboratory.

Substances such as milk, paint, ink, air, and muddy water are mixtures. The atoms, molecules, or other particles in a mixture are intermingled, but they have not combined with each other and undergone chemical changes. Unlike compounds, mixtures do not have definite composition; hence their composition cannot be described by a fixed formula.

Mixtures can usually be separated by physical methods, such as chromatography, evaporation, distillation, or filtration. The choice of method depends largely on the nature of the mixture and the type of substances it contains.

SOLUTIONS

A true solution is a mixture of two or more different substances that cannot be separated by settling, filtering, or other mechanical means.

In the case of a water-and-sugar solution, for instance, the sugar will not settle to the bottom of the glass nor can it be removed by filtering. When going into solution, the sugar crystals break up into tiny particles called molecules. These sugar molecules become evenly distributed among the water molecules so that a uniform liquid results.

Solutions differ from substances known as colloids. When particles dissolve to form a solution, they break up into individual molecules or ions, whereas colloid particles consist of clusters of molecules. Fog, smoke, milk, and gelatin are familiar examples of colloids.

In solutions the solvent, frequently a liquid, is the substance in which another substance dissolves. The dissolved substance is called the solute. It may be a solid (as in the sugar solution), a liquid (as when alcohol and water are mixed), or a gas. Mixtures of two solids, as when two metals are combined in an alloy (such as copper and zinc combined to form brass), are sometimes called solid solutions.

Some substances that form solutions break down into particles finer than molecules. In a solution of common table salt and water, for example, many of the salt molecules are divided into fragments called ions—an atom or group of atoms with a positive or negative electric

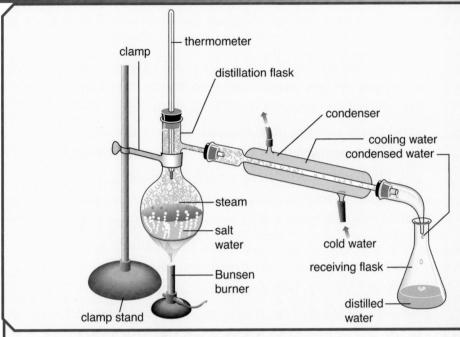

This distillation apparatus shows a simple distillation of salt water. In the distillation flask, salt water is heated to its boiling point, producing water vapor, while the salt remains in the liquid solution. The water vapor rises through the top of the flask and passes into the condenser, a glass tube that sits within a larger tube. Cold water flows through the space between the tubes, cooling the water vapor in the inner tube so that it condenses back into liquid water and flows into the receiving flask. © Merriam-Webster Inc.

charge. Chief among the substances that form ionized solutions are acids, bases, and salts. Ionized solutions conduct electricity and are very active chemically. They are known as solutions of electrolytes, while solutions composed of molecules that do not bear an electric charge are solutions of nonelectrolytes.

To break down an electrolyte into ions, the solvent must have a strong ability to decrease the forces of attraction and repulsion of the charged particles. Water is the most common

65

solvent for electrolytes. (The ocean itself is an example of an electrolyte solution.) Among the other substances used as solvents for electrolytes are ammonia and sulfur dioxide.

The amount of a substance that can be dissolved in a given quantity of solvent is a measure of the substance's solubility. This ability of a solute to dissolve in a solvent depends primarily on the chemical properties of both substances. Temperature also often affects solubility, and pressure sometimes does. The solubility of solids almost always increases when the solvent is heated. For example, more than twice as much sugar will dissolve in a quantity of boiling water as will dissolve in the same amount of ice-cold water. On the other hand, the solubility of gases decreases as the temperature of the solvent rises. When solids or liquids go into solution, they raise the boiling point of the solvent and lower its freezing point.

The solubility of one liquid in another may be partial or complete. The strength, or concentration, of a solution is commonly indicated by a percentage. A 5 percent salt solution indicates that the solution contains 5 parts by weight of salt to 95 parts by weight of water.

When a liquid at a given temperature has dissolved all of a substance that it can hold, the solution is said to be saturated. Ordinarily, as a hot, saturated solution of a solid cools, some of the dissolved substance comes out of solution and resolidifies, forming crystals on the side of the container or dropping to the bottom as a precipitate. In certain cases the surplus remains in solution after the liquid has cooled, creating a supersaturated solution. Jarring or agitating the liquid or dropping a fragment of the dissolved material into it will usually cause the surplus material to solidify suddenly.

Solutions are involved in most chemical reactions and play an essential role in life processes. Air, for example, is a solution of oxygen and nitrogen with small amounts of other gases. Oxygen taken into the lungs goes into solution in the blood, unites chemically with the hemoglobin in red blood cells, and is released to body tissues. Chemical industries take advantage of the properties of solutions for many processes, including separation and purification. Many common inorganic chemicals, for example, are obtained by extracting crystals out of a water solution.

MOLECULES AND CHEMICAL FORMULAS

Elements vary from those that are highly active to those that are almost completely inert. The tendency of an atom to combine is

a chemical property of the atom, and it is controlled by electrical forces at the atomic level. Those forces forge the links, called chemical bonds, that hold two or more atoms together. The groups of atoms formed by chemical bonding are known as molecules. Molecules are the smallest units of a compound that can exist while still keeping the substance's composition and chemical properties.

To make elements and their combinations easier to describe in written form, chemists commonly indicate each element with an abbreviation called a chemical symbol. This is usually the initial or the first two letters of the common name or the Latin name of the element. Chemists use such shorthand to represent not only the name of an element but also one atom of that element. The symbols for single atoms of hydrogen, carbon, and iron, for example, are H, C, and Fe.

Atoms of one element can combine with each other to form molecules. For example, atoms of oxygen (O), hydrogen (H), nitrogen (N), and chlorine (Cl) tend to react with their own kind to form two-atom molecules. These molecules are represented by the abbreviations O_2, H_2, N_2, and Cl_2 respectively. The subscript 2 shows that two atoms of the element make up one molecule of the element. Oxygen also can form a three-atom molecule called ozone that

FORMATION OF OZONE

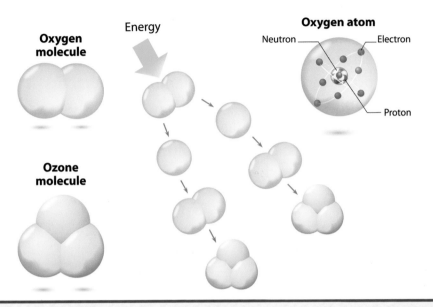

Oxygen molecule

Energy

Ozone molecule

Oxygen atom

Neutron

Electron

Proton

The oxygen people breathe is a molecule that is made of two oxygen atoms. Ozone molecules have three oxygen atoms. Ozone absorbs much of the sun's ultraviolet radiation and helps to shield living things on Earth from severe ultraviolet-radiation damage. Designua/Shutterstock.com

has the abbreviation O_3. Abbreviations of molecules written in this way are known as chemical formulas. They show both the kinds of atoms and the number of each kind in the molecule.

Six gaseous elements—helium, neon, argon, krypton, xenon, and radon—were thought to be completely inactive chemically when they were first discovered and so were named inert gases. All are present in the air as single, uncombined atoms; thus in their gaseous forms their symbols (for example, He for helium) are written without subscripts. Since the early 1960s chemists have found that under proper conditions at least some of them can be made to form compounds. Today the preferred name of this family of elements is noble gases.

Chemical formulas are also used to represent compounds and their molecular compositions. One atom each of hydrogen and chlorine react

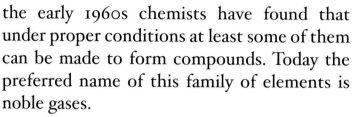

CHEMICAL EQUATIONS

To express the reactions that form and break down molecules, chemists write chemical equations. These are shorthand versions of ordinary word descriptions, and they make use of symbols and formulas for elements and compounds. For example:

Word description: Two molecules of hydrogen react (or combine) with one molecule of oxygen to form two molecules of water.

Chemical equation: $2H_2 + O_2 \rightarrow 2H_2O$

Word description: Two molecules of ammonia break down (or decompose) to form one molecule of nitrogen and three molecules of hydrogen.

Chemical equation: $2NH_3 \rightarrow N_2 + 3H_2$

In chemical equations, the substances on the left side of the arrow—those undergoing the chemical change—are called reactants. The substances on the right side—the result of the reaction—are called products. The arrow can be read as "give," "form," or "yield."

to form the compound hydrogen chloride. The chemical formula for hydrogen chloride is HCl. Hydrogen atoms combined with carbon atoms in a proportion of four to one form the flammable gas methane, which is represented as CH_4. Three atoms of chlorine combine with one atom of aluminum (Al) to form aluminum chloride ($AlCl_3$), which in a hydrated form (combined with molecules of water) is used in antiperspirants.

In reading chemical formulas, it is important to keep in mind what they do not show. Formulas usually say little about the chemical bonding of the atoms. In addition, they are necessarily written "flat" on paper or a chalkboard, although molecules actually exist in three dimensions in space. For example, the formula for methane, CH_4, does not show that all four hydrogen atoms are attached only to the carbon atom, or that the hydrogen atoms are arrayed in space around the carbon atom at equal distances and angles. Thus the molecule resembles a tetrahedron, or four-sided pyramid (including the base), with the carbon atom at the center and the hydrogen atoms at the corners. In solving chemical problems—such as designing a new plastic, for example—chemists often must consider the geometric structures of the molecules that will react and the molecules that will be produced.

CHAPTER 5

INORGANIC COMPOUNDS AND BONDS

The modern idea of the nature of a chemical compound—a single substance containing fixed proportions of two or more elements—was adopted early in the 19th century. The number of known compounds then was growing fast as chemists learned to separate and analyze the substances found in nature. To organize and simplify the facts concerning these compounds, they classified those obtained from living organisms—plants and animals—as organic and all others as inorganic. This seemed especially logical as long as no one knew how to convert any

In 1828, the German chemist Friedrich Wöhler synthesized an organic chemical, urea, out of inorganic chemicals and helped to launch the field of organic chemistry. SSPL/Getty Images

compound of either class into any compound of the other. Many scientists believed that the formation of organic compounds required the action of some unidentified vital force that could be exerted only by living things.

In 1828 the German chemist Friedrich Wöhler made the organic compound urea by heating the inorganic compound ammonium cyanate. He thereby proved that no vital force is needed, but the idea continued to affect the thinking of some chemists for many years. By the time the concept was abandoned, the division of chemical compounds into organic and inorganic had become permanent. All of the organic compounds contain carbon, but very few of the inorganic ones do, so the definition of organic compounds was changed to conform to this fact: any compound of carbon is an organic compound except carbon monoxide, carbon dioxide, carbonates, cyanides, cyanates, thiocyanates, and certain carbides.

Of all the chemical elements found in nature, the atoms of all but two of them (helium and neon) form compounds by combining with atoms of other elements. There are two main kinds of forces, or chemical bonds, that hold atoms together in compounds: covalent and ionic.

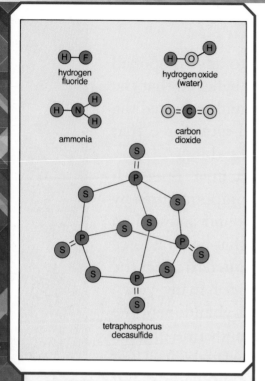

Single and double lines represent single and double covalent bonds for the compounds hydrogen fluoride (HF), hydrogen oxide (H$_2$O), ammonia (NH$_3$), carbon dioxide (CO$_2$), and tetraphosphorus decasulfide (P$_4$S$_{10}$). Encyclopædia Britannica, Inc.

COVALENT BONDS

A covalent bond forms when two atoms attract the same pair of electrons, which is said to be shared. A covalent bond affects only two atoms, but most atoms can form more than one covalent bond at a time. The compound hydrogen fluoride consists of molecules in which one atom of hydrogen and one atom of fluorine are held together by a covalent bond. Atoms of oxygen or sulfur, however, form two covalent bonds in many of their compounds. Atoms of nitrogen or phosphorus form three or five. Two atoms can share two or three pairs of electrons, forming double or triple covalent bonds.

IONIC BONDS

Covalent bonds are not formed between atoms that differ greatly in their attraction for electrons. In these cases, the atom with the stronger attraction completely removes one or more electrons from the other. The atom that gains electrons becomes a particle with a negative electric charge, and the atom that loses electrons becomes positively charged. The charged particles are called ions, and the electrical attraction between oppositely charged particles is the force called the ionic, or electrovalent, bond. This bond differs from the covalent bond

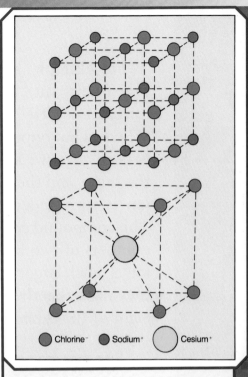

Ionic bonds, represented here by broken lines, hold positively charged sodium (top) or cesium (bottom) ions in a matrix of negatively charged chloride ions, and vice versa. Encyclopædia Britannica, Inc.

because a positive ion attracts every negative ion in its vicinity. The reverse is also true. Instead of forming molecules in which each bond affects only two nearby atoms, ions of opposite charge pack closely together, forming arrangements in which each kind is surrounded by the largest possible number of the other kind. For any combination of positive and negative ions, the possibilities are limited by their relative sizes and charges.

For example, the compound sodium chloride (table salt) consists of positive sodium ions and negative chloride ions. Their charges are equal but opposite, so there are equal numbers of the two kinds. Their sizes are nearly the same, and they pack together so that each ion is surrounded by six of the other kind. The compound cesium chloride also has equal numbers of two kinds of ions, but the cesium ion is much larger than the chloride ion. When they pack together, each ion is surrounded by eight of the other kind.

MAKING A COMPOUND

In making a new compound, the chemist first selects substances that seem likely to combine in the desired way and decides on a procedure for carrying out the reaction. In most cases one or more of the starting materials will be solids, and reactions between such materials are ordinarily very slow because only the atoms at the surface can be approached by atoms of another compound. The most convenient way to speed a chemical reaction is to dissolve all the starting compounds in a liquid solvent. Water was long the only solvent used for this purpose. It dissolves a great number of inorganic compounds, and it is inexpensive and not poisonous.

Water is not always satisfactory, however, because many compounds do not dissolve in it. In other cases, it reacts with the starting materials or with the desired product. Therefore, chemists have studied the use of other substances as solvents and have found several that are suitable. Ammonia and sulfur dioxide, which are gases at ordinary temperatures and pressures, can be liquefied without great difficulty. They are not as cheap as water, and they are poisonous, but they can be handled safely and recovered to be used again. They dissolve many compounds that are not soluble in water. Chemists have found that many compounds, organic as well as inorganic, can be produced by reactions that take place in these solvents but not under other conditions.

IMPORTANT INORGANIC COMPOUNDS

Several inorganic compounds that are widely used in the chemical industry and other activities have become known in commerce as "heavy" chemicals. They get this name because such great quantities of them are produced every year.

SULFURIC ACID

Sulfuric acid leads the list of heavy chemicals. Each year many millions of tons of this compound are made and used in the manufacture of fertilizers, detergents, dyes, fibers, and petroleum products.

The principal method now used for making sulfuric acid is called the contact process. Sulfur is first burned, which combines it with oxygen from the air to form a mixture of the gas sulfur dioxide and unchanged air. This mixture is then brought into contact with solid substances that act as catalysts, speeding the reaction of sulfur dioxide with additional oxygen to form sulfur trioxide. The contact between the gases and the catalysts, which are not affected by the reaction, takes place during the essential step that gives its name to the whole process. Finally sulfuric acid is formed by combining sulfur trioxide with water. Represented in chemical symbols, the whole process looks like this:

$$S + O_2 \rightarrow SO_2$$
sulfur oxygen sulfur
dioxide

$$2SO_2 + O_2 \rightarrow 2SO_3$$
sulfur oxygen sulfur
dioxide trioxide

$$SO_3 + H_2O \rightarrow H_2SO_4$$
sulfur water sulfuric
trioxide acid

The ores of many metals are sulfur compounds. In the conversion of these ores to the pure metals, the sulfur must be removed. Usually this step is carried out by heating the ore in the presence of air. The sulfur in the ore combines with oxygen from the air to form sulfur dioxide. In modern ore refineries, the sulfur dioxide cannot be allowed to escape because it is a dangerous pollutant. Instead, it is collected and used for making sulfuric acid by the contact process.

SODIUM CHLORIDE

Sodium chloride is the basis of a whole family of inorganic heavy chemicals. The chief source of sodium chloride is the mineral called halite, or rock salt, which is found in large deposits in the northeastern United States and elsewhere.

Several industrial processes are used to transform sodium chloride into sodium hydroxide (also called caustic soda), sodium carbonate

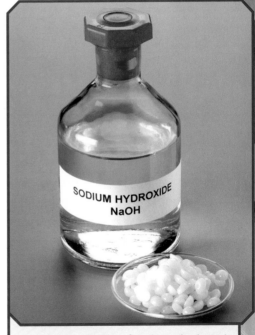

A reagent bottle of sodium hydroxide solution and pellets of sodium hydroxide are probably the most frequently used base, or alkali, for driving chemical reactions or neutralizing acidic materials in laboratories and industrial processes. Martyn F. Chillmaid/Science Source

(soda ash), calcium chloride, chlorine, sodium, sodium sulfate, sodium bisulfate, hydrochloric acid, sodium cyanide, and sodium hypochlorite. Hydrogen is not present in sodium chloride, but large amounts of it are produced and collected when sodium hydroxide and chlorine are made by passing a direct current of electricity through brine, a solution of sodium chloride in water. This process is the most important industrial application of electrochemistry.

HYDROCHLORIC ACID

Without a constant supply of hydrochloric acid, many of the nation's businesses would shut down. Hydrochloric acid is a solution of hydrogen chloride gas (HCl) in water. About 1,000 cubic feet (30 cubic meters) of this gas can be dissolved in 1 cubic foot (0.03 cubic meters) of water. For commercial use hydrochloric acid is usually marketed as a solution containing 28 to 35 percent hydrogen chloride by weight.

Some of the main industrial uses of hydrochloric acid are the cleaning, or pickling, of metals, the production of glucose and corn sugar from starch, and the refining of cane sugar. It is also used in making glue and gelatin and is essential in the manufacture of synthetic rubber and plastics.

There are three principal commercial methods of manufacturing hydrochloric acid. First, hydrogen chloride is obtained as a by-product in the chlorination of hydrocarbons. This is how much of the hydrochloric acid is produced in the United States. In the second process, sulfuric acid and salt are roasted to form hydrogen chloride. In the third method, hydrogen chloride is produced by the combustion of hydrogen in chlorine.

Gaseous hydrogen chloride is colorless and has a pungent, irritating odor. The water solution is yellow in color because of impurities, usually dissolved iron. Hydrogen chloride gas is soluble in some organic solvents. Hydrochloric acid reacts with many metals to form salts known as chlorides. Hydrochloric acid is secreted in gastric juices by glands in the walls of the stomach, where the acid aids in the digestion of foods. Small quantities of hydrochloric acid occur in nature in the gases given off by active volcanoes and in waters from volcanic mountain sources.

In the 18th century, scientists called hydrochloric acid muriatic acid, from the Latin word meaning "pickled." During the early 19th century, hydrogen chloride was a waste product of various industrial processes, such as the production of soda ash. Until its many industrial uses were realized, it was dissolved in liquids and dumped at sea.

If the sodium chloride is melted—by heating it to about 1,475 °F (800 °C)—rather than dissolved in water, electric current causes chlorine to form at one electrode and metallic sodium to form at the other.

NITROGEN COMPOUNDS

Ammonia and nitric acid are also heavy chemicals. They are made from nitrogen gas, which can be obtained by separating it from oxygen and the other gases that are present along with nitrogen in the atmosphere. Ammonia is produced when nitrogen combines with hydrogen, but this reaction can be made to take place rapidly only if the pressure on the mixture of gases is raised to about 1,000 times that of the atmosphere, the temperature is raised to about 1,290 °F (700 °C), and a catalyst (such as iron) is present.

$$N_2 + 3H_2 \rightarrow 2NH_3$$
nitrogen hydrogen ammonia

The theoretical and technological problems that had to be solved before this process could be carried out on an industrial scale were so difficult that Nobel Prizes were awarded to two German chemists who carried out the research and development. Most of the ammonia now produced is used, either by itself or mixed with other compounds, as fertilizer. Large amounts of ammonia are also used in the chemical industry.

One of the major industrial uses of ammonia is the manufacture of nitric acid. This process, which is like the contact process that is used in making sulfuric acid, consists of several distinct reactions. Ammonia does not burn easily in air, but it will combine with the oxygen in the air if a mixture of air and ammonia is passed through a red-hot screen made of platinum wire. The platinum is a catalyst. The product of the reaction is another gas called nitric oxide. The nitric oxide combines with additional oxygen in the air to form nitrogen dioxide. Nitric acid finally is formed when the nitrogen dioxide reacts with water. In this step more nitric oxide also forms, but it is quickly converted back to nitrogen dioxide because of air. Nearly all the nitric acid produced is used in making other chemical products. It combines with ammonia to form ammonium nitrate, which is used as an explosive and a fertilizer.

The reaction of nitric acid with the organic compound glycerol forms glyceryl trinitrate (commonly called nitroglycerin). With toluene, nitric acid forms trinitrotoluene (TNT). These compounds are both powerful explosives.

CHAPTER 6

ORGANIC COMPOUNDS AND BONDS

Carbon unites with many elements to form a great variety of compounds that are found in such substances as coal, petroleum, fabrics, plastics, and rubber. Other carbon compounds include plant and animal tissues, sugars, proteins, starches, and cellulose. About 1 million carbon compounds are known. The substances that contain carbon are called organic compounds, and the science that deals with them is known as organic chemistry.

Carbon compounds exist in such number and variety because of the chemical properties of carbon. Carbon has four valence electrons that form covalent bonds. Since carbon is in group 14 (IV A) of the periodic table, it appears to be midway between the metals and nonmetals and has the ability to react with both types of elements. The structure of the carbon atom is unique among atoms, allowing a great array of compounds that are stable under normal

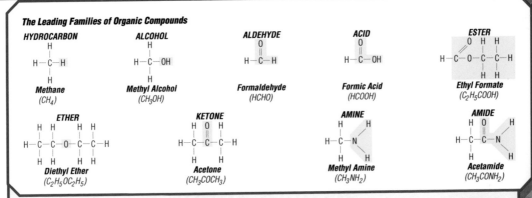

The Leading Families of Organic Compounds

HYDROCARBON — Methane (CH_4)

ALCOHOL — Methyl Alcohol (CH_3OH)

ALDEHYDE — Formaldehyde (HCHO)

ACID — Formic Acid (HCOOH)

ESTER — Ethyl Formate (C_2H_5COOH)

ETHER — Diethyl Ether ($C_2H_5OC_2H_5$)

KETONE — Acetone (CH_3COCH_3)

AMINE — Methyl Amine (CH_3NH_2)

AMIDE — Acetamide (CH_3CONH_2)

These examples are the leading types of organic compounds. Each type has a characteristic grouping of atoms that identifies it; and all can be considered as derived from the hydrocarbon methane. For example, substitution of the hydroxyl group (–OH) for a hydrogen atom in a methane yields an alcohol (this and other characteristic groups are shown in colored boxes). Substitution of a double-bond oxygen atom for two hydrogen atoms of an alcohol gives an aldehyde. Addition of another oxygen atom to an aldehyde yields an organic acid. Encyclopædia Britannica, Inc.

atmospheric conditions and reactive in other situations. Carbon reacts as follows:

1. Carbon atoms have the unusual property of combining with each other to form rings or long chains. No other element does so as extensively.

2. Carbon will combine with many different atoms or groups of atoms. This property, together with the ability to form long chains, makes carbon the most versatile of all elements in forming compounds.

3. Carbon forms many compounds that exist as isomers. Isomers are molecules

with the same number and kinds of atoms, but in different arrangements—for example, CH_3CHCl_2 and CH_2ClCH_2Cl.

THE FAMILY OF HYDROCARBONS

The effects produced by these factors can be illustrated with the most simple organic compounds, called hydrocarbons—meaning compounds containing hydrogen and carbon

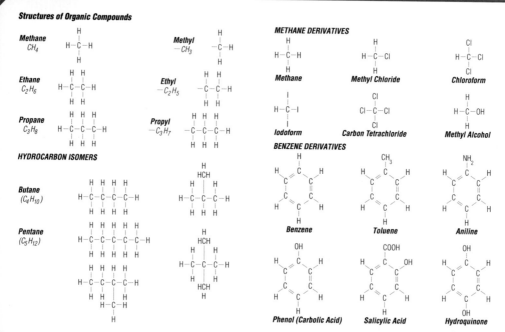

Some of the simplest hydrocarbons are shown here, with formulas of both molecular and structural type indicated. Encyclopædia Britannica, Inc.

only. This type of compound can be shown by molecular formulas, which state the kind and number of atoms in the compound, or by structural formulas. Structural formulas show the covalent bonds that hold the atoms together, with a short bar for each bond. In such a formula, each bar represents a pair of electrons; usually each atom concerned contributes one of the electrons in the bond, as follows:

Electrons in the bond: $\overset{\rightarrow}{\underset{\leftarrow}{C:H}}$ The bond shown by a bar: $C-H$

Groups of atoms can also be combined by one or more covalent bonds. Such groups (sometimes called radicals) offer at their ends one or more covalent bonds for making compounds. Radicals from simple parent hydrocarbons are named by changing the ending of the name of the hydrocarbon from which they are derived, thus: meth*ane*, CH_4 (the hydrocarbon); meth*yl*, CH_3 (the radical).

Hydrocarbons form many derivatives; that is, compounds in which the hydrogen atoms are replaced by other atoms or groups. Several methane derivatives in the image on the bottom of page 86 show such replacements. Isomers also form derivatives, thus adding to the host of compounds.

HYDROCARBONS OF THE BENZENE TYPE

Hydrocarbons of the open-chain type are found typically in petroleum. Coal tar is another important source of hydrocarbons; but most hydrocarbons from coal tar have the carbon arranged in rings rather than in chains. The rings usually have six carbon atoms. The simplest of these hydrocarbons is benzene (C_6H_6). The importance of benzene and benzene derivatives can be judged by listing a few with their uses in modern life:

- Benzene—a powerful solvent; usable for motor fuel
- Toluene—used to make explosives such as TNT
- Aniline—an important material for dyes
- Phenol (carbolic acid)—a strong antiseptic
- Salicylic acid—basis of drugs such as aspirin
- Hydroquinone—photographic developer
- Chlorobenzene—used to make insecticides
- Dodecylbenzene—used to make detergents

Compounds with ring structures are called aromatic compounds, whereas those with chain structure are called aliphatic compounds.

COMPOUNDS WITH DOUBLE AND TRIPLE BONDS

Aromatic compounds differ from many aliphatic hydrocarbons in the type of bonds that hold the molecules together. In a chain-structure molecule, such as methane, the carbon atom forms one bond (consisting of a shared pair of electrons) with each of four other atoms. In such situations, the carbon is said to be tetravalent. Since four is the largest number of atoms with which a carbon atom can join, such compounds are said to be saturated.

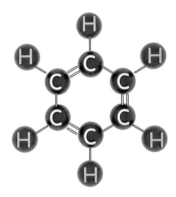

Benzene is the simplest aromatic compound and contains the benzene ring of six carbon atoms bonded to each other in a ring structure with each of the carbon atoms attached to a hydrogen atom by a covalent bond. booblik_uk/iStock/Thinkstock

Benzene, however, has only six hydrogen atoms combined with six atoms of carbon. Each carbon atom therefore only uses one valence bond to hold a hydrogen atom. The other three bonds join with other carbon atoms to form the benzene ring, and every other bond between the carbon atoms must be double. To form this bond, the carbon atoms share two pairs of electrons, thus: C::C. A double bond can also be shown with two bars: C=C. A triple bond can be shown with three bars: C≡C.

Double bonds can occur in chain-type compounds as well as in those of the ring type. Compounds having such bonds are said to be unsaturated because elements such as hydrogen, chlorine, and bromine can open the bonds and saturate the four carbon valences by adding atoms of these elements. Two unsaturated chain-type hydrogen carbons, ethylene and acetylene, are shown, together with the end results of saturating them with hydrogen atoms:

Ethylene (C_2H_4)

$$\begin{array}{cc} H & H \\ | & | \\ H-C & = C-H \end{array}$$

$$C_2H_4 + H_2 \rightarrow C_2H_6$$

Ethane

Acetylene (C_2H_2)

$$H-C \equiv C-H$$

$$C_2H_2 + 2H_2 \rightarrow C_2H_6$$

Ethane

CLASSIFICATION OF CARBON COMPOUNDS

The study of compounds of carbon has been organized in much the same way as the study of the elements; that is, by grouping them into families. All organic compounds can be grouped into a small number of families. Moreover, these families can be considered to be derivatives of the hydrocarbon methane (CH_4).

Just as a family of elements in the periodic table has similar properties, so does a family of organic compounds. This similarity arises from the properties of some characteristic group in each family. In the examples shown, the characteristic group is attached to the group called methyl (CH_3) in the alcohol, ketone, amine, and amide; with a hydrogen atom (H) in the aldehyde and acid. The ethyl groups (C_2H_5) are in the ether and ester. The characteristic group can react with the characteristic group of other compounds to form new compounds.

Organic chemists have learned how to use the properties of each characteristic group to make new compounds. Hence they can make many new derivatives of a given compound. Organic chemists can design a formula, then make the compound that corresponds to that formula.

MANY KINDS OF ALCOHOLS

Most people have heard of wood alcohol (CH_3OH), called methyl alcohol or methanol, and grain alcohol (C_2H_5OH), called ethyl alcohol or ethanol. Such simple alcohols have a carbon chain with the characteristic hydroxyl (–OH) group at one end, and H or a hydrocarbon radical at the other end. Alcohols may have more than one OH group. Two examples of such alcohols are the following:

Ethylene glycol

Glycerin

Ethylene glycol is called a dihydric alcohol, from the two OH groups. Glycerin is trihydric. Alcohols can also be of the branched-chain type, with hydrocarbon radicals at each side of the carbon chain instead of at one side, as in ethylene glycol or glycerin. An example is

This woman is creating a soda/glycerin/castile soap solution as she formulates environmentally friendly cleaning products in her home. Glycerin is used as a solvent, moisturizer, pharmaceutical agent, and sweetening agent. Fort Worth Star-Telegram/ MCT/Getty Images

isopropyl (rubbing) alcohol. It has the same molecular formula (C_3H_7OH) as normal propyl alcohol.

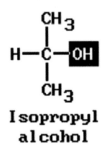

Isopropyl
alcohol

ALDEHYDES, KETONES, AND ETHERS

Aldehydes are formed when alcohols are partially oxidized. The most familiar and simplest aldehyde is formaldehyde (HCHO), which is obtained mainly from the vapor-phase oxidation of methanol, or methyl alcohol. Formaldehyde is used as an embalming fluid, as an animal specimen preservative for biological work, as a disinfectant, and as an important raw material for the preparation of Bakelite and other plastics.

Ketones are formed when such branched-chain alcohols as isopropyl ($CH_3CHOHCH_3$) are partially oxidized. Removal of two hydrogen atoms leaves one carbon atom united by a double bond to one oxygen atom, as in an aldehyde. Acetone (CH_3COCH_3) is one of the best-known ketones. Ketones are highly reactive compounds, though they are less so than aldehydes. They are used primarily as solvents for lacquers.

Ethers may be formed from two molecules of an alcohol in this manner:

$$C_2H_5O \boxed{H} \atop C_2H_5 \boxed{OH} \quad + H_2SO_4 \rightarrow C_2H_5OC_2H_5 + H_2SO_4 \text{ (Hydrate)}$$

The sulfuric acid (H_2SO_4) removes a molecule of water (H_2O), shown in black, and allows the C_2H_5 and C_2H_5O to join together, with $-O-$ in the middle. Diethyl ether ($C_2H_5OC_2H_5$) is used as an anesthetic.

TWO TYPES OF ORGANIC ACIDS

Organic acids are of two types. One has the COOH group (the carboxyl group). An example is acetic acid (CH_3COOH), the acid in vinegar. It is made by oxidizing grain alcohol or by the fermentation of the fruit sugar in cider.

The other type has a phenol group, as in phenol (C_6H_5OH).

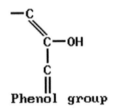

Phenol group

Each type appears in salicylic acid (OHC_6H_4COOH). Water solutions of each type are weakly acidic. The solutions can be neutralized with alkali; this forms salts of the organic acids.

ESTERS, AMINES, AND AMIDES

Ripe fruits—especially bananas, oranges, and pineapples—owe their odors to the presence of esters. Some common esters formed with acetic acid (CH_3COOH) are found in the following list:

NAME	FORMULA	FOUND IN
Ethyl acetate.........	$CH_3COOC_2H_5$	....
Butyl acetate.........	$CH_3COOC_4H_9$	bananas
Amyl acetate..........	$CH_3COOC_5H_{11}$	bananas
Octyl acetate.........	$CH_3COOC_8H_{17}$	oranges
Ethyl butyrate........	$C_3H_7COOC_2H_5$	pineapple

Amines are formed when a hydrogen atom is replaced with an NH_2 group. Simple replacements appear in such examples as methylamine (CH_3NH_2), from the aliphatic hydrocarbon methane, and aniline ($C_6H_5NH_2$), from the aromatic hydrocarbon benzene. Amides are formed when the −OH of the carboxyl group in an organic acid is replaced—for example, acetamide (CH_3CONH_2). Amines and amides are intermediates in forming other compounds. For example, aniline is a basis for many dyes.

COMPOUNDS WITH DOUBLE-ACTING GROUPS

These "family" groups enter into a tremendous variety of combinations in plant and animal life and in a host of other chemical processes. Many of the combinations are possible because many compounds have more than one family group. A good example is glycine.

$$H-\underset{\displaystyle \underset{NH_2}{|}}{\overset{\displaystyle \overset{H}{|}}{C}}-COOH$$

Glycine

Glycine is called an amino acid because it has both an acid group (COOH) and an amino group (NH_2), which acts as a base. Each group can combine with its chemical opposite. Thus glycine can join end to end with itself and with other basic or acidic compounds.

As shown by earlier formulas, salicylic acid has a carboxyl group (COOH) and a hydroxyl group (OH). Either or both groups can join with compounds in forming drugs or other compounds.

CHEMICAL CHARACTERISTICS OF FATS

Many such combinations are found in fats, carbohydrates, and proteins. Fats are esters of glycerin and higher acids such as palmitic ($C_{15}H_{31}COOH$), oleic ($C_{17}H_{33}COOH$), and stearic ($C_{17}H_{35}COOH$). A typical molecule of fat shows in black what has been removed from the acid and the glycerin to form the ester, or fat:

$$
\begin{array}{ccc}
\text{C}_{17}\text{H}_{35}\text{CO}\;|\text{OH}| & \text{H}|\text{--O--}\overset{\overset{\textstyle H}{|}}{\underset{}{\text{C}}}\text{--H}| & \text{C}_{17}\text{H}_{35}\text{COOCH}_2 \\[4pt]
\text{C}_{17}\text{H}_{33}\text{CO}\;|\text{OH}|\;+ & \text{H}|\text{--O--}\overset{}{\underset{}{\text{C}}}\text{--H}|\;\longrightarrow & \text{C}_{17}\text{H}_{33}\text{COOCH} + 3\text{H}_2\text{O} \\[4pt]
\text{C}_{15}\text{H}_{31}\text{CO}\;|\text{OH}| & \text{H}|\text{--O--}\underset{\underset{\textstyle H}{|}}{\overset{}{\text{C}}}\text{--H}| & \text{C}_{15}\text{H}_{31}\text{COOCH}_2
\end{array}
$$

Acid   Glycerin   Ester

Treating the ester with a base (such as sodium hydroxide, NaOH) restores the glycerin and adds three Na ions to the acid radicals, giving three molecules of soap ($3C_{17}H_{35}COONa$). Such a process occurs in the upper intestine in digesting fats. The digestion products then move into the bloodstream and are carried to the body cells to be resynthesized to body fats or to be oxidized, producing carbon dioxide, water, and energy. In the oxidation process, fat produces twice the energy of carbohydrates or protein.

CARBOHYDRATES AND PROTEINS

Photosynthesis in plants produces carbohydrates (sugars, starch, cellulose). Plant sugar ($C_6H_{12}O_6$) is formed from carbon dioxide and water. The molecular formula is the same for either of two simple sugars:

$$
\begin{array}{c}
\text{OH OH OH H O OH} \\
| \quad | \quad | \quad | \quad \parallel \quad | \\
\text{H—C—C—C—C—C—C—H} \\
| \quad | \quad | \quad | \quad \quad | \\
\text{H H H OH H}
\end{array}
\qquad
\begin{array}{c}
\text{OH OH OH H OH O} \\
| \quad | \quad | \quad | \quad | \quad \parallel \\
\text{H—C—C—C—C—C—C—H} \\
| \quad | \quad | \quad | \quad | \\
\text{H H H OH H}
\end{array}
$$

Fructose Glucose

The total units H and OH are present in numbers sufficient to form six molecules of water ($6H_2O$); hence the name carbohydrates, meaning "hydrate of carbon." The molecules differ only in the position of the C=O unit. They both have several alcohol units, but glucose is an aldehyde and fructose is a ketone. If an OH is removed from one such molecule and an H from another, the molecules can join at the vacated bonds. The sugar sucrose ($C_{12}H_{22}O_{11}$), used for sweetening food, is formed in this way.

If 25 or 30 simple sugar units are joined, they form a molecule of starch $(C_6H_{10}O_5)x$. A mass of 100 to 3,000 joined together is a molecule of cellulose $(C_6H_{10}O_5)y$.

HELPFUL VITAMINS AND DRUGS

Body cells have the ability to absorb the digested fats, proteins (amino acids), and carbohydrates (glucose) and convert them into parts of the cell to replace damaged or worn portions or to build additional cells. To do this work properly, the cells require help from catalysts, which they are unable to produce. These are called vitamins.

Drugs likewise are helpful because they interact in definite chemical ways with tissues and the course of bodily processes. Because interactions are often so delicate, a slight variation in a drug molecule can have a profound effect upon its action. A good example of this is afforded by the group of sulfa drugs that are derived from the original sulfanilamide as follows:

Each sulfa at the right and left is made by substituting its chain for the H marked with an arrow in the parent drug, sulfanilamide.

The framework of all living cells and tissues is made of protein, and the many different kinds of protein are all made of amino acids linked together in long chains or large globules. The amino acids are linked, as already explained for glycine, by means of the acidic COOH and the basic NH_2 radicals. Fats may also be included in cell tissue.

During digestion, proteins are broken down by enzymes into amino acids and other parts. These fragments are absorbed and recombined into body proteins as needed, or they may be oxidized to supply energy.

SYNTHETICS— FIBERS, PLASTICS, AND RUBBER

Organic chemists have learned to produce a host of valuable synthetic substances. Generally the chemist selects a suitable molecule or molecules with double-acting properties and unites

Synthetic polymers are generally either plastics or fibers. Most plastics can be molded easily and are flexible.
© iStockphoto.com/richterfoto

101

(polymerizes) them into a network of very large molecules called polymers. Polymers consist of large chains that separate when enough heat is supplied so that they slip apart. When cooled, they become firmly entangled again. Among the products made from polymers are synthetic fibers: rayon, nylon, polyester, acrylic, and acetate. Substances called plastics are shaped into objects using a variety of processes. Synthetic rubbers can be toughened by a process called vulcanization.

CHAPTER 7

THE HISTORY OF CHEMISTRY

Modern chemistry is only about two centuries old. The earlier history of chemistry may be divided into three periods: magic, alchemy, and "primitive modern," a period of transition between alchemy and truly modern chemistry.

THE PERIOD OF MAGIC

The period of magic extended from prehistoric times to about the beginning of the 1st century CE. Most people believed that natural processes were controlled by spirits, and they relied on magic to persuade the spirits to help while they conducted practical operations. Very little progress was made toward understanding how the universe is made, but much practical knowledge was gathered. Perhaps 9,000 years ago, people devised reliable techniques for making and sustaining fire. Gradually they learned to use fire to harden pottery, extract metals from ores, make alloys, and develop

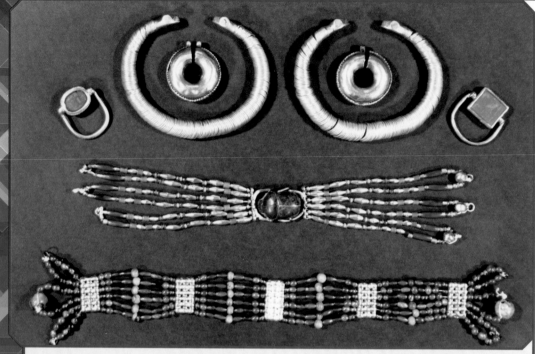

Ancient Egyptian jewelry from the tomb of King Tutankhamen was fashioned from gold, precious stones, and colored glass. Such jewelry was believed to help the dead in the afterlife, and gold was thought to be divine because it resembled the sun. Photos .com/Thinkstock

materials such as glass. Certain elements that occur naturally in a pure state, such as gold, copper, and sulfur, were recognized and valued for their properties. This was the period of the Sumerian, Babylonian, Egyptian, and Greek cultures.

About 400 BCE the Greek philosopher Democritus theorized that all matter was made up of tiny, indivisible units he called atoms, but his idea was not based on scientific evidence. Other Greek philosophers, including Thales and Aristotle, also speculated on the nature of matter, though their theories, too, had little in common with modern chemical knowledge. They believed that earth, air, fire, and water (some imagined a fifth substance called "quintessence") were the basic elements of all matter. They speculated on the possibility of removing such qualities as hardness, heat or cold, and color from common materials and combining them to make rarer or more valuable substances. They knew that iron could be drawn from a dirty, brown earthen rock and that bronze was made by combining copper and tin. Therefore it seemed possible that if yellowness, hardness, and other qualities could be properly combined, the product would be gold. Such speculations gave rise to alchemy.

THE STERILE PERIOD OF ALCHEMY

The span of time from about the beginning of the 1st century CE to about the 17th century is considered the period of alchemy. The alchemists believed that metals could be converted into gold with the aid of a marvelous mineral called the philosopher's stone, which they never succeeded in finding or making. They did discover new elements, and they invented basic laboratory equipment and techniques

An alchemist works in his shop. The objectives of alchemy were to discover a substance called the philosopher's stone, which was thought to transform common metals such as lead into silver or gold, and to find an "elixir of life," a cure for diseases and a way to extend life. In a private collection

that are still used by chemists. However, the alchemists learned very little that was worthwhile concerning the fundamental nature of matter or of chemical behavior. They failed because their basic theories had almost nothing to do with what actually happens in chemical reactions.

In the 13th century such men as Roger Bacon, Albertus Magnus, and Raymond Lully began to realize how futile it was to search for the philosopher's stone. They suggested that alchemists might rather seek to help the world with useful new products and methods.

In the 16th century, another important leader in the new trend was Theophrastus Bombastus von Hohenheim, an aggressive, talented Swiss who used the Latin name Paracelsus. He insisted that the object of alchemy should be the cure of the sick. The elements, he said, were salt, sulfur, and mercury (long connected with the "elixir of life," another nonexistent alchemical substance), and they would give health if present in the body in the proper proportions. On this basis he practiced medicine and attracted many followers. Thus began iatrochemistry, or chemistry applied to the study of medicine and the treatment of disease.

One of the first scientific chemists was Robert Boyle. In 1660 he helped found one of the first scientific organizations in Europe, the Royal Society of London. In a book called *The Sceptical Chymist* (1661) he rejected previous theories of the composition of matter and compiled the first list of the elements that are recognized today. He also discovered the relationship between the volume and the pressure of a gas.

THE BEGINNINGS OF MODERN CHEMISTRY

For about two centuries after Boyle, scientists continued to make useful discoveries but made little progress in understanding the true nature of matter or chemical behavior. Perhaps the greatest source of confusion and defeat in these centuries was a theory of burning (combustion) called the phlogiston theory. It was originated by the German chemists Johann Joachim Becher and Georg Ernst Stahl in the late 1600s. According to this theory, phlogiston, an "essence" like yellowness or hardness in the theories of the ancient philosophers, escaped from substances during the burning process. By this time, chemists were learning to gain knowledge the modern way: by testing theories with experiments. But such tests failed to confirm the existence of phlogiston.

The first clue to a more useful theory came when an English chemist, Joseph Priestley, discovered in 1774 that a gas (now known as oxygen) was essential to the burning process. (Oxygen was also discovered by the Swedish chemist Carl Wilhelm Scheele at about the same time.) A few years earlier another English scientist, Henry Cavendish, had identified hydrogen as an element. The French chemist Antoine-Laurent Lavoisier used the discoveries of Priestley and Cavendish in a series of experiments from which he formulated the presently accepted theory of combustion. He also showed that burning, the rusting of metals, and the breathing of animals are all processes in which oxygen combines chemically with other substances. Lavoisier's most significant finding was that the products of a chemical reaction have the same total mass as the reactants, no matter how much the substances are changed. This means that, even when chemical changes take place, something essential stays the same. These contributions are often considered to mark the beginning of modern chemistry.

DALTON'S THEORY OF ATOMS

Lavoisier's results gave chemists their first sound understanding concerning the nature of chemical reactions. The next milestone was the atomic theory, advanced in 1805 by an English schoolteacher, John Dalton. This theory states that matter is made up of small particles called atoms, that each chemical element has its own kind of atoms (in contrast to earlier ideas that atoms are essentially alike), and that chemical changes take place between atoms or groups of atoms. To support his theory Dalton set about calculating the relative weights of the atoms of several elements. The Swedish chemist Jöns Jacob Berzelius greatly expanded this work in a long series of experiments in which he found accurate atomic weights for about 40 elements. He also found chemical

John Dalton formulated an atomic theory to explain chemical reactions based on the concept that the atoms of different elements vary in shape and size. SSPL/Getty Images

formulas for most of the inorganic compounds known at that time.

Equipped at last with sound views about the nature of matter and of chemical reactions, chemistry made rapid advances. About 1811 came the hypothesis of Amedeo Avogadro, an Italian chemist, about the number of molecules in a given volume of gas. To Dalton's theory that the atoms of a single element all have the same weight, Avogadro added the following notions: that equal volumes of different gases at the same temperature and pressure contain the same number of molecules, and that some of the gaseous elements are found in two-atom molecules rather than as independent atoms.

THE RISE OF ORGANIC CHEMISTRY

The vast new field of organic chemistry was opened in 1828 with Friedrich Wöhler's synthesis of urea, a compound present in certain body fluids of mammals, from inorganic materials in his laboratory. This disproved the assumption that such compounds could be formed only through the operation of a "life force" present in animals and plants. About this time chemists also began to realize that

a molecule's geometric structure had a great effect on its chemical and biological properties.

The German chemist Friedrich Kekulé showed in 1858 that carbon atoms can combine with four other atoms and link with each other to form long chains. He also proposed the cyclic (ring) structure of benzene about this time. Another important field, electrochemistry, was born in the 1830s when Michael Faraday formulated its laws.

MORE NEW FIELDS OF INVESTIGATION

By the middle of the 19th century, about 60 elements were known. A few chemists had noticed that certain elements were much alike in their properties and saw a pattern emerge when elements were arranged according to atomic weight. The work of these men enabled the Russian chemist Dmitry Mendeleyev, in 1869, to publish the first periodic table. Mendeleyev predicted correctly that the gaps left in his table would be filled by as yet undiscovered elements with properties that he also predicted. This table became the foundation of theoretical chemistry.

To this period belongs Robert Bunsen, whose most important contribution to chemistry was the organization of the field of spectroscopy, based on observations that each element when heated emits light having a characteristic color, or wavelength. To aid his research, he invented many instruments, including the spectroscope and the Bunsen burner.

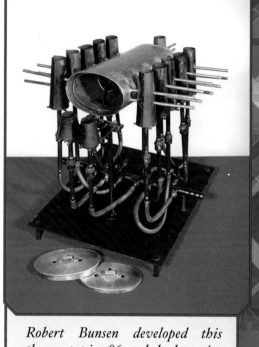

Robert Bunsen developed this thermostat in 1867 to help determine the specific gravity of vapors and gases by maintaining a steady temperature within an enclosure. SSPL/Getty Images

In the second half of the 19th century, Louis Pasteur, who had done his research on isomers as a young man, became interested in how yeast and bacteria are involved in chemical reactions and in causing illness. He invented the process of pasteurization to prevent foods and beverages from spoiling, and he proved that microorganisms are responsible for the chemical changes called fermentation in beer and wine and for several diseases of humans and other animals. He was also the first to use vaccines against anthrax, chicken cholera, and rabies. His

113

achievements helped lay the groundwork for both biochemistry and microbiology.

THE DEVELOPMENT OF PHYSICAL CHEMISTRY

The area where physics and chemistry overlap, which had been explored by Avogadro in his investigations of gas volumes, became prominent in the last quarter of the 19th century. Wilhelm Ostwald and Jacobus van't Hoff used physical principles to describe the energy changes accompanying reactions in solution that go on simultaneously in opposite directions (reactants to products and products to reactants). Svante August Arrhenius proposed the idea that compounds such as acids and bases form ions (electrically charged particles) when they dissolve in water and that these ions allow the solutions to conduct electricity.

The American chemist Willard Gibbs developed the "phase rule," a mathematical formula showing how temperature and pressure affect the capacity of substances to exist in equilibrium in as many as three different states of matter, or phases (solid, liquid, and gas). Accurate atomic weight determinations were the work of Theodore Richards. Between 1894 and 1898, the efforts of the chemist William Ramsay and the physicist Lord Rayleigh (John William Strutt) resulted in the isolation of helium on Earth (the element previously had been detected in the sun) and the discovery of the other noble gases.

After 1900, chemists began receiving invaluable aid from discoveries made in physics about the electrical nature of the atom. Henry Moseley, working with X-rays emitted from atoms of the different elements, reorganized the elements using atomic number—a quantity equal to the positive charge of the atomic nucleus—rather than atomic weight. Max von Laue and Sir William Bragg and his son Lawrence Bragg laid the basis for determining the atomic structure of substances in crystal form by means of X-rays. Francis W. Aston developed the mass spectrograph, a device that separates atoms or molecular fragments of different mass, and used it to discover isotopes of many elements. Later Harold C. Urey isolated deuterium, an isotope of hydrogen with one neutron. Deuterium has become important as a chemical tracer, in thermonuclear weapons, and in fusion power research.

NUCLEAR CHEMISTRY AND ATOMIC STRUCTURE

In 1896 Henri Becquerel with Marie Curie and Pierre Curie discovered the phenomenon of radioactivity. Thus, other scientists were shown that atoms were not permanent and changeless, and the basis was laid for nuclear chemistry and nuclear physics.

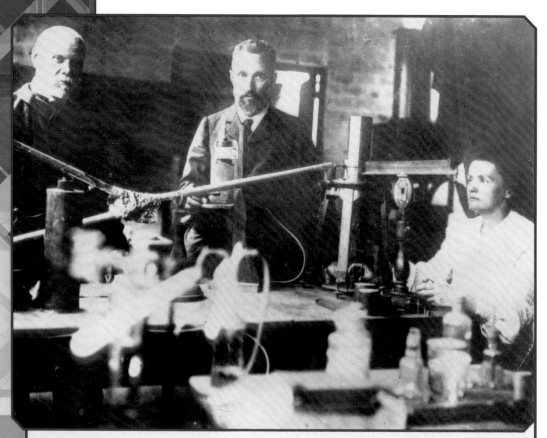

French physicists Marie Curie (right) and Pierre Curie (center), and French chemist Gustave Bémont (left) work in a laboratory. The Curies, with Bémont's assistance, discovered the radioactive elements radium and polonium in uranium ore. Photos.com/Thinkstock

Having found that atoms sometimes transmuted into other elements on their own, scientists attempted to do the same in the laboratory. In 1919 Ernest Rutherford became the first to succeed, using natural radioactivity to transmute nitrogen atoms into atoms of oxygen and hydrogen. In 1934 Frédéric and Irène Joliot-Curie made radioactive isotopes of elements that were not normally radioactive. Five years later Otto Hahn, Fritz Strassmann, and Lise Meitner discovered that the uranium nucleus could be made to fission, or split into the nuclei of lighter elements, by bombarding it with uncharged particles called neutrons.

By the early 1940s nuclear reactions had been used to make radioactive isotopes of all elements; Glenn Seaborg contributed much to this work. In the 1940s and 1950s Seaborg and his coworkers also made several elements not known to exist in nature. The new elements had atomic numbers greater than 92, the atomic number of uranium. By the early 21st century nuclear scientists were adding new elements to the periodic tale with atomic numbers higher than 110.

Rutherford's discovery in 1911 that the atom has a tiny massive nucleus at its center allowed chemists and physicists such as Gilbert Lewis,

Irving Langmuir, and Niels Bohr over the next 20 years to explain chemical bonding and atomic structure in terms of the behavior of electrons orbiting the nucleus. In the late 1920s and early 1930s, Linus Pauling contributed much to knowledge of the nature of the chemical bond and of the relationship between the structure of atoms and molecules and their properties.

NEW SYNTHETIC MATERIALS

Some of the most notable achievements in modern chemistry have come from efforts to create whole new classes of materials. Early plastics such as celluloid, invented in the late 1860s, relied on large molecules found in natural substances. In 1909, however, the Belgian-born inventor Leo H. Baekeland took out a United States patent for a hard, chemically resistant, electrically nonconductive plastic that he called Bakelite. Made from the chemical combination of synthetic compounds called formaldehydes and phenols, Bakelite proved to be exceptionally useful as an electrical insulator and as a structural material for such consumer goods as radio cabinets, telephone housings, and even jewelry.

The commercial success of Bakelite sparked great interest and investment in the plastics industry, in the study of coal-tar products and other organic compounds, and in the theoretical understanding of complex molecules. These research activities led not only to new dyes, drugs, and detergents but also to the successful manipulation of molecules to produce dozens of materials with particular qualities such as hardness, flexibility, or transparency.

Another dramatic result of the growth in chemical knowledge has been the expansion of the modern pharmaceutical industry. Notable early achievements include the development of the synthetic drugs acetylsalicylic acid (aspirin) in 1897, Salvarsan (for treating the bacterial disease syphilis) in 1910, and Prontosil (the first sulfa drug for treating bacterial infections) in 1932, as well as the discovery of the antibiotic penicillin (produced naturally by a mold) in 1928.

Since the late 20th century the rapid growth in the understanding of chemical processes in general, and of organic and biochemical reactions in particular, has revolutionized the treatment of disease. Most drugs available today do not occur naturally but are made in the laboratory from elements and inorganic and organic compounds. Others are derived from animals, plants, microorganisms, and minerals, by pharmaceutical researchers who often use chemical reactions to modify molecular structures to make drugs that are more effective and have fewer harmful side effects.

CHEMISTRY FOR A NEW MILLENNIUM

Two special focuses of the chemical industry in the 21st century are based on innovations stemming from the phenomenon of

superconductivity (the ability to conduct electricity with no resistance) and the discovery of a new form of carbon.

In 1986 two Swiss chemists discovered that lanthanum copper oxide doped with barium became superconducting at the "high" temperature of 35 K (-238 °C, or -397 °F). Since then, new superconducting materials have been discovered that operate well above the temperature of liquid nitrogen—77 K (-196 °C, or -321 °F). In addition to its purely scientific interest, much research focuses on practical applications of superconductivity.

In 1985 Richard Smalley and Robert Curl at Rice University in Houston, Tex., collaborating with Harold Kroto of the University of Sussex in Brighton, England, discovered a fundamental new form of carbon, possessing molecules consisting solely of 60 carbon atoms. They named it buckminsterfullerene (later nicknamed "buckyball"), after Buckminster Fuller, the inventor of the geodesic dome. Research on fullerenes has accelerated since 1990, when a method was announced for producing buckyballs in large quantities and practical applications appeared likely. In 1991 *Science* magazine named buckminsterfullerene their "molecule of the year."

Two centuries ago, Lavoisier's chemical revolution could still be questioned by the English émigré Joseph Priestley. A century ago, the physical reality of the atom was still doubted by some. Today, chemists can maneuver atoms one by one with a scanning tunneling microscope, and other techniques of what has become known as nanotechnology are in rapid development. The history of chemistry is an extraordinary story.

CONCLUSION

Over the ages, giant strides have been made in scientists' understanding of how the world is put together and how it works. Many scientific disciplines overlap with chemistry to some extent. Biochemists, chemists with knowledge of biology and medicine, have successfully synthesized life-saving medications in the laboratory. They have also learned how DNA regulates chemical reactions in the human body and, in some cases, how to repair or replace damaged DNA structure. Molecular biologists use their knowledge of chemistry to search for ways to combat antibiotic-resistant bacteria. Physical chemists, chemists with a good understanding of physics, invented the battery and continue to look for ways of developing new types, such as by coating clothing material with a chemical that can use sunlight to power electronics. Other physical chemists might work in businesses that manufacture cosmetics, or they may study how to make nuclear power plants safer and more efficient. As scientific disciplines

The Israeli biochemist *Ada E. Yonath was awarded the 2009 Nobel Prize in Chemistry, along with American scientists Venkatraman Ramakrishnan and Thomas Steitz, for her work in studying the structure and function of cellular particles called ribosomes.* Dan Porges/Archive Photos/Getty Images

overlap more and more, who knows what chemicals and principles scientists will discover next? In the meantime, your growing knowledge of basic chemistry will help you better understand the world you live in and allow you to make educated decisions to make it even better.

atom The basic building block of elements.

catalyst A substance that increases the rate of a chemical reaction without being changed by the chemical reaction.

colloid Substance that contains clusters of molecules suspended in another substance.

compound Substance that contains more than one type of atom joined together by chemical bonds.

electron A negatively charged subatomic particle found outside the nucleus of an atom.

element A substance composed of only one type of atom.

functional group Individual element or group of atoms that reacts as a unit.

ion An atom or group of atoms with a positive or negative charge.

isotope An atom of the same element that contains a different number of neutrons.

mass The amount of matter in an object.

matter Anything that takes up space and has volume.

neutron A neutral subatomic particle found in the nucleus of an atom.

nucleus The dense, central core of an atom that contains protons and neutrons.

precipitate A solid that forms as a result of a chemical reaction.

proton A positively charged subatomic particle found in the nucleus.

qualitative analysis A process used to determine which types of elements or groups of elements exist in a chemical sample.

quantitate analysis A process used to establish how much of a particular element or group of elements exist in a chemical sample.

solution A mixture of two substances that cannot be separated by ordinary mechanical means.

sublimation The transition from the solid phase directly to the gaseous phase without going through the liquid phase.

synthesis The process in which two or more substances combine to form a new compound.

valence electrons The outermost electrons that are most often involved in chemical reactions.

weight Measurement of the force of gravity acting on an object.

FOR MORE INFORMATION

American Association for the Advancement
   of Science (AAAS)
1200 New York Avenue NW
Washington, DC 20005
(202) 326-6400
Website: http://www.aaas.org
The AAAS provides lesson plans, activities,
   and online tools, including podcasts, and
   a database of volunteer subject experts
   to help teachers feed students' interest
   in science.

The American Chemical Society (ACS)
1155 Sixteenth Street NW
Washington, DC 20036
(800) 227-5558
Website: http://www.acs.org
The ACS coordinates chemistry-related
   summer internship programs and
   provides excellent educational material, including the award-winning
   ChemMatters magazine.

Chemical Heritage Foundation
315 Chestnut Street
Philadelphia, PA 19106
(215) 925-2222

Website: http://www.chemheritage.org

The Chemical Heritage Foundation maintains media collections designed to preserve the history of chemistry-related sciences. Its online resources include profiles of women in chemistry, modern chemical innovators, and chemistry in history.

The Chemical Institute of Canada
130 Slater Street, Suite 550
Ottawa, ON K1P 6E2
Canada
(888) 542-2242
Website: http://www.cheminst.ca

The CIC sponsors many hands-on chemistry competitions for secondary students, including the It's Chemistry, Eh?! YouTube Contest, the National Crystal Growing Competition, and the Canadian Chemistry Olympiad.

Council for Chemical Research
1550 M Street NW, Suite 1200
Washington, DC 20005
(202) 429-3971
Website: https://www.ccrhq.org

The Council for Chemical Research provides information and profiles about companies, universities, and organizations actively engaged in cutting-edge chemical research.

Environmental Protection Agency (EPA)
1200 Pennsylvania Avenue NW
Washington, DC 20460
(202) 272-0167
Website: http://www.epa.gov
The EPA's website contains articles, quizzes, and homework resources for students who are interested in finding out more about how chemicals impact the environment and human health.

WEBSITES

Because of the changing nature of Internet links, Rosen Publishing has developed an online list of websites related to the subject of this book. This site is updated regularly. Please use this link to access the list:

http://www.rosenlinks.com/SCI/Chem

Angelo, Joseph. *Quantifying Matter*. New York, NY: Facts On File, 2011.

Bateman, Graham, ed. *Introducing Chemistry: Atoms, Molecules, and States of Matter* (Facts at Your Fingertips). London, UK: Brown Bear Books, 2011.

Brown, Theodore L., H. Eugene LeMay Jr., Bruce E. Bursten, Catherine J. Murphy, and Patrick M. Woodward. *Chemistry: The Central Science*. 12th ed. Boston, MA: Prentice Hall, 2012.

Buckley, Don. *Introduction to Chemistry*. Boston, MA: Pearson Education, 2010.

Clowes, Martin. *The Basics of Organic Chemistry* (Core Concepts). New York, NY: Rosen Publishing, 2014.

Cobb, Cathy, and Monty Fetterolf. *The Joy of Chemistry: The Amazing Science of Familiar Things*. Amherst, NY: Prometheus Books, 2010.

Coelho, Alexa, and Simon Quellen Field. *Why Is Milk White? & 200 Other Curious Chemistry Questions*. Chicago, IL: Chicago Review Press, 2013.

Curran, Greg. *Homework Helpers: Chemistry*. Pompton Plains, NJ: Career Press, 2011.

Dingle, Adrian. *How to Make a Universe with 92 Ingredients: An Electrifying Guide to the Elements*. Toronto, ON: Owlkids Books, 2013.

Etingoff, Kim. *Women in Chemistry* (Major Women in Science). Broomall, PA: Mason Crest, 2013.

Gray, Leon. *The Basics of the Periodic Table* (Core Concepts). New York, NY: Rosen Publishing, 2014.

Gray, Theodore. *The Elements: A Visual Exploration of Every Known Atom in the Universe*. New York, NY: Black Dog & Leventhal Publishers, 2012.

Gray, Theodore. *Theo Gray's Mad Science: Experiments You Can Do At Home—But Probably Shouldn't*. New York, NY: Black Dog & Leventhal Publishers, 2012.

Green, Dan. *The Elements*. New York, NY: Scholastic, 2012.

Gregersen, Erik, ed. *The Britannica Guide to the Atom* (Physics Explained). New York, NY: Britannica Educational Publishing and Rosen Educational Services, 2011.

Gregersen, Erik, ed. *The Britannica Guide to Matter* (Physics Explained). New York, NY: Britannica Educational Publishing and Rosen Educational Services, 2011.

Horton, Michael. *Take-Home Chemistry: 50 Low-Cost Activities to Extend Classroom Learning*. Arlington, VA: NSTA Press, 2011.

Jackson, Tom. *The Basics of Atoms and Molecules* (Core Concepts). New York, NY: Rosen Publishing, 2014.

Kean, Sam. *The Disappearing Spoon and Other True Tales of Madness, Love, and the History of the World from the Periodic Table of the Elements*. New York, NY: Little, Brown and Company, 2010.

Moore, John. *Chemistry for Dummies*. Hoboken, NJ: John Wiley & Sons, 2012.

Stewart, Ian. *The Handy Chemistry Answer Book*. Canton, MI: Visible Ink Press, 2014.

VanCleave, Janice Pratt. *Step-by-Step Science Experiments in Chemistry*. New York, NY: Rosen Publishing, 2012.

Wolny, Phil. *Chemical Reactions* (Science Made Simple). New York, NY: Rosen Publishing, 2011.